NOW WHAT?

A STEP-BY-STEP APPROACH TO LAND YOUR NEW JOB OR CAREER

KIRSTEN BRUMBY

WHY NOT HAVE KIRSTEN BRUMBY AS A GUEST SPEAKER ON YOUR PODCAST, OR AT YOUR NEXT CONFERENCE, CORPORATE TRAINING SEMINAR OR EVENT?

KIRSTEN BRUMBY – CONNECTING PEOPLE TO PURPOSE

E: info@kirstenbrumby.com
W: www.kirstenbrumby.com
Linkedin: www.linkedin.com/in/kirsten-brumby

When you need *the* leading voice in HR and recruitment systems, the leading expert in job applications and interview skills, someone to make writing policies and procedures seem easy, Kirsten Brumby is the source.

After co-founding a consulting firm that generated seven-figures annually, Kirsten Brumby has spent over 20 years coaching, training and consulting for individuals, teams and organizations.
▶ She has facilitated initiatives in leadership
▶ Small business
▶ Not for profit boards
▶ Career and life coaching
▶ Internationally across industries including corporate and government

BOOKS BY KIRSTEN BRUMBY

Now What?
A Step-By-Step Approach to Land Your New Job or Career

When embarking on a new career or applying for a new job it is extremely hard to stand out from the crowd.

This book provides clarity about that next step. Kirsten guides you to:

- Explore what you really want, whether that's to leave your current job, or start a new career
- Learn the steps to find clarity and make a decision
- Make your resume stand out from the crowd
- Write cover letters and selection criteria responses that make your application irresistible and become the person who shines at that interview

How to Write Effective Policies and Procedures
The System that Makes the Process of Developing Policies and Procedures Easy

- A step-by-step guide to do-it-yourself policies and procedures from the self-confessed policies and procedures pragmatist. Kirsten has nailed the task that many of us dread and now shares her secrets.

Online Programs By Kirsten Brumby

▶ How to Write the Right Resume and Cover Letter
▶ How to Write the Job Application and Meet Selection Criteria (Secure that interview)
▶ How to Be Outstanding in a Job Interview
▶ How to Get Clarity About Your Next Career Move

www.whatnowcareer.com/resources
www.kirstenbrumby.com

NOW WHAT?

A STEP-BY-STEP APPROACH TO LAND
YOUR NEW JOB OR CAREER

KIRSTEN BRUMBY

The Potentialist
by *Maggie White*

Mind Potential Publishing

Copyright © 2020 Kirsten Brumby

ALL RIGHTS RESERVED. No part of this book may be reproduced or transmitted in any form whatsoever, electronic, or mechanical, including photocopying, recording, or by any informational storage or retrieval system without the expressed written permission from the author and publisher.

Author: Kirsten Brumby
Title: Now What?
ISBN Paperback: 978-1-922380-30-2
ISBN Kindle: 978-1-922380-32-6
Category: Business (career) | Self-Help Techniques

 A catalogue record for this book is available from the National Library of Australia

Publisher: Mind Potential Publishing
Division of Mind Design Centre Pty Ltd,
PO Box 6094, Maroochydore BC Queensland, Australia, 4558.
International Phone: +61 405 138 567
Australia Phone: 1300 664 544
www.thepotentialist.com | www.kirstenbrumby.com

Cover design by: NGirl Design | www.ngirldesign.com.au

LIMITS OF LIABILITY | DISCLAIMER OF WARRANTY: The author and publisher of this book have used their best efforts in preparing this material and they disclaim any warranties, (expressed or implied) for any particular purpose. The information presented in this publication is compiled from sources believed to be accurate at the time of printing, however the publisher assumes no responsibility for omissions or errors. The author and publisher shall not be held liable for any loss or other damages, including, but not limited to incidental, consequential, or any other. This publication is not intended to replace or substitute medical or professional advice, the author and publisher disclaim any liability, loss or risk incurred as a direct or indirect consequence of the use of any content.

Mind Potential Publishing bears no responsibility for the accuracy of the information provided as either online or offline links contained in this publication. The use of links to websites does not constitute an endorsement by the publisher. The publisher assumes no liability for content or opinion expressed by the author. Opinions expressed by the Author do not represent the opinion of Mind Potential Publishing or Mind Design Centre Pty Ltd.

Printed in Australia

DEDICATION

This book is dedicated in the main to my partner Steve. He has provided unstinting encouragement and support over many years for me to follow my own path and answer my own 'Now What?' questions as they have arisen. He has willingly sat beside me on what he calls my career rollercoaster. Reassuring me on the way up, holding my hand when I'm too scared to look at the drop, and sharing the exhilaration of the ride.

And to my parents, Linda and Allan – who, when asked, have never been able to answer the question of what it is I do for a living, but have always wanted me to be happy doing it.

CONTENTS

Foreword	2
Introduction	5
Step 1: Prepare yourself to think differently	13
Step 2: Clarity to start talking	25
Step 3: Seek and Search – The numbers game	39
Step 4: Your Resume – Rewrite your history	59
Step 5: Writing applications – It's not about you, it's about them	71
Step 6: Landing that job or career with a great interview – Be your best you	89
Step 7: The Secret Ingredients – Persistence, perseverance and preparation	109
Your 'Now What?' Answered	121
Acknowledgments	123
Meet the Contributor	124
References and Recommended Reading	125
Meet the Author	126
What Others Have to Say	128

FOREWORD

For over 20 years I have had the privilege of positively influencing thousands of people's careers through my work in the world of career transition. I understand and have seen firsthand the struggles, concerns, the disappointments, hopes and dreams that jobseekers experience at all stages of their career. I enjoy seeing the flush of success and satisfaction when someone comes to a place of certainty about their next career move. According to the Bureau of Labor Statistics, the average worker holds approximately ten different jobs before the age of forty. Forrester Research predicts that today's younger workers may hold up to twelve to fifteen jobs in their lifetime.

One of the major career challenges people face today is when their current position no longer meets their needs, they often move swiftly from one unsatisfactory job to the next without first pausing to reflect and solve the challenge of exactly 'which' job or career will best align with their skills, passion and need for a sense of purpose.

People more often than not try to change themselves to fit the next job, instead of making the time and taking the right steps to find the job or career that fits them and their lifestyle needs.

In her book 'Now What?', Kirsten Brumby not only answers the many questions I've heard jobseekers ask time and time again, but she also provides step-by-step strategies and a fresh approach to every stage that people go through when embarking on a path to find the right job for them.

For those too, who seek more than just 'the right job', but are considering a complete career change, Kirsten provides the exact steps to define 'what's next,' and to find a resolution to the question, *"what will I do now?"*

This book is a testament to Kirsten's depth of understanding and experience in this field. She establishes a clear path for the reader to employ empathy as a foundational skill that can be used to great effect in all stages of career transition. She takes into account every step you'll need, from innovative approaches in the search for a suitable position, through to an effective strategy for ensuring the application process is easy, helping you understand how to meet selection criteria and of course, to enhance your success at getting that interview and employing winning interview skills essential to your success.

Throughout the book, Kirsten provides the reader with the exact 7 Steps they need to decide what they want to do next. She then systematically guides the reader through a step-by-step process toward getting exactly what they want, infused with stories and case studies of those who have taken this path.

The 7 Steps also provide an easy reference point for anyone struggling with a particular part of the job-application process. Kirsten outlines her unique approach; and provides you with the exact exercises you'll need, and the steps that make you and your application stand out from the crowd.

Now What? is like having your own career coach. Kirsten is with you every step of the way; she supports and guides you with expert advice, and the step-by-step systems that will enhance your chances of success, build your confidence and help you to take ownership of your future career.

Alison Hernandez
Director, Randstad Risesmart APAC

INTRODUCTION

If you find yourself at a career crossroads and have been asking yourself the question 'Now What?' in relation to your next job or new career and you feel disheartened or discouraged, unhappy or hopeless then this book is exactly what your career doctor ordered.

If you are questioning your ability or even dealing with a fully-fledged crisis of confidence, this book will help reframe your thoughts, feelings and beliefs and improve the skills you need to land a job or choose your next career move. It enables you to make a sustained and ultimately effective effort to make the right decision and succeed.

There are many stories behind this book, and there is a real person behind every story. The first person you will meet is me, and this story is my own.

Kirsten's Story

Some years ago, in a career far away, I was an Information Technology professional of 10 years and found myself suddenly unemployed due to insolvency of the company I worked for. I was also four months pregnant.

I wasn't concerned, I was full of self-confidence and I made an immediate 3-step plan.

1. I'd walk into a lucrative three-month 'fill-in' contract until my baby was ready to be born
2. I'd have a few months off when the baby arrived, and then
3. I'd come back and get another job immediately when the baby was ready to be left in care…

INTRODUCTION

I could have it all...

Easy, right?

I wasn't worried at all – I had great skills, an outstanding breadth and depth of experience, and the market at the time was buoyant with all kinds of IT jobs. So, I boldly re-entered the job-seeking world looking for that three-month contract to fulfil step 1 of my plan. (At that time, it was eight years since I'd last had to search or apply for a job or be interviewed.)

>
> *For the next 60 days, I was focused and determined, and worked hard at the job of finding a job.*
>

Things had changed in those eight years

For the next 60 days, I was focused and determined, and worked hard at the job of finding a job.

I updated my resume, spent umpteen hours searching for jobs, and many more hours writing cover letters and answering selection criteria.

In all I applied for 55 jobs, and in return received – nothing, nada!

- ▶ No interviews
- ▶ No feedback
- ▶ No job
- ▶ Just a big fat nothing

I felt depressed and increasingly desperate as the time ticked by and the tally of job applications grew.

Worse still, I felt my confidence in my capabilities slipping as each day went by and each application went unanswered. If so many people were not offering me an interview, did that mean I wasn't up to the job?

As my confidence dropped even further, I started applying for jobs well below my ability...

> ▶ I was blown away; I didn't get an interview for these either

I was no longer confident

On the very last job I applied for, I was eventually offered an interview. Unfortunately, it was a six-month contract and by then it was too late in my pregnancy to accept the interview.

My strike rate was 55 job applications equaled one offer of an interview for a contract it was now too late to fulfil!

> *My strike rate was 55 job applications equaled one offer of an interview for a contract it was now too late to fulfil!*

It was then that I gave up looking and entered self-funded maternity leave. I had funded the past months of my job search, now I faced the financial strain of no income or entitlements for support.

Plus, I was totally devoid of any hope that I would be able to get a job when returning after the baby.

As you can imagine, I was enormously stressed, utterly despondent and felt jaded by the job search and recruitment experience. In reality, my capability hadn't changed – in my field I was highly competent.

INTRODUCTION

> Looking back, once my wounded confidence was out of the way, the reality was my skills, experience and capability in Information Technology was not the problem, the problem was that I wasn't skilled at doing *these* five jobs:
>
> - ▶ I wasn't good at understanding the recruitment process
> - ▶ I hadn't understood what was required for a stand-out resume
> - ▶ I knew nothing back then about writing an amazing job application
> - ▶ I didn't know how to put my resume at the top of the pile by meeting selection criteria
> - ▶ I didn't get a chance to learn how to shine at an interview (because after 55 applications, I still didn't get to attend an interview at all)

Back then, the big thing for me was that I had failed at something I set out to do – I had not landed a job.

Although the next nine months saw me busy with a new baby and my existing toddler, I had the mind-space for reflection. I allowed myself time for feelings to bubble to the surface, and I faced the hard reality that I had failed.

I was angry with 'recruiters' (any, and all, of the people involved in the recruiting process). At the time, I blamed recruiters for their incompetence. It was clear to me that…

- ▶ They were no good at reading applications
- ▶ They ignored or didn't know how to recognize potential
- ▶ They didn't know how to choose the right person to put forward for the job

And the greatest offense as far as I was concerned,

> ▶ They placed no importance on communication with job applicants.

For a time, I felt they were the primary reason behind my misery and failure during the process. And while I have been able to temper this judgement over the years, a simmering irritation still remains, which I'll get to later in the book.

> 66
>
> *perhaps my lack of competency lay with showing others, or communicating to them, that I could do the job.*
>
> 99

During the nine months I took off, I was offered part-time work with the company I had just been with, as they'd had the opportunity to trade out of insolvency. My self-confidence in my job capabilities returned as soon as I started work again and I realized if I was competent at work, but had not been able to land a job, then perhaps my lack of competency lay with showing others, or communicating to them, that I could do the job.

So, it wasn't *all* the recruiter's fault – I could admit I had a hand in my own failure

I began to see what it was that I had failed at on multiple levels. I was driven to work out why I had failed, after all, I still needed a job when returning to the workforce after maternity leave.

My failure presented me with surprising gifts

This experience had presented me with the opportunity (although not by choice) to pause before launching myself at the next job and consider whether that was what I *really* wanted.

INTRODUCTION

> This opportunity to learn, to assess what I wanted, to then improve my job search and application systems and strategies, led me to a brand-new career.

Looking back, if I had somehow managed to land a job, any job (which was what I was looking for), among those 55 applications, perhaps this new career I've created that has helped so many others, would never have happened.

That period also became the basis for the insights in this book about the recruitment process.

These insights drove me to consider what I could do differently, and importantly, to find a way for a job applicant to have some control over a process where, in the past, it may have felt hopeless. I was able to move to a place where I didn't feel beholden to others (namely recruiters), who are not always as experienced or capable in the tasks they need to carry out.

When I became ready to return to work, I had already made the decision that it wasn't a new job I sought…

I was ready to significantly change my career direction

I selected, and applied for only one job, and, using the techniques I describe later in this book, landed it even though it was not in Information Technology or a related field.

My first important step on my way to a new career was:

- ▶ I answered my very own 'Now What?' and was ready to take that next step.

> *I answered my very own 'Now What?' and was ready to take that next step.*

For the past 15 years, I've coached clients and organizations through this same process, some of whom you will get to know through their stories in this book.

Throughout this book, my aim is to coach you through this process, because it's hard to see what's really needed when you're in the thick of it. When you're in it (as I was all those years ago), you are too busy doing the work, thinking about what to do now, searching for jobs and writing applications. Worrying why the phone hasn't rung or no one has returned your emails and phone calls.

You are far too caught up in riding the wave of emotion that comes with the process. That's where the support from this book comes in.

You'll notice that throughout the book, I offer you steps, not traditional chapters. I do this because there is a step-by-step system to your next job or career move. It's a system that turns the traditional job search on its head. It starts with you, not the job, the resume or the application or interview. They come next… first, the art of 'Now What?', begins with you!

So, I invite you to come on the journey, seeking certainty in your next job or career choice. The journey of your very own, 'Now What?'

Kirsten Brumby

STEP 1
Prepare yourself to think differently

Following my 55-job application spree, my reflections led me to realize that the greatest mistake I made in my quest for a job, was that I jumped in feet first, frantically looking for jobs and shooting off applications left and right. I worked hard all right, but I never once stopped to seriously consider what was going wrong. When I finally accepted defeat, because my baby was so close to being due that I couldn't even take a possible contract, I was able to recognize the top mistakes that had undermined my valiant efforts.

1. I never considered my *thinking* could be so completely wide of the mark. I presumed what I was *doing* needed tweaking – I just had to write a better application, I had to find more jobs to apply for.

2. I didn't employ one shred of empathy. Everything I did, what I wrote, what I said, was all centered on *me*, not on the recruitment agent, not on the organization hiring, or even the person doing the hiring.

3. Because of my financial concerns, I took the misguided and short-term view that I *must* get a job, *any* job, right now.

Now, as a coach to others who are trying to decide on a new career or apply for a job, I find many people make the same mistakes. When you're able to spend a little time at the start, before jumping into anything, thinking a little differently, then the action you take will be more targeted to what you actually want to achieve.

Let's take a deeper look at each of my errors in thinking, so that you don't make the same mistakes I did!

> *Getting a job has its own set of skills particular to the process of searching, applying for, and landing a job.*

1. **Getting a Job is the skill set you need**

   My flawed thinking was, because I was good at my job, I should be able to get a job easily. This thinking could not have been further from reality. Knowing you have the skills and experience to make a great employee, has no bearing whatsoever on the process of getting a job as that employee.

   - Getting a job has its own set of skills particular to the process of searching, applying for, and landing a job.

   - The bad news is that unless you 'luck into' landing that job (for example, you know the recruiter and they like you), you need to be good at some of these skills – and the better you are at them, the better your chances of landing the job. And quite honestly, some of the skills involved are not really relevant in any other sphere.

   - For example, unless you want to become a career coach or a recruitment agent, the particular skill of writing a contemporary, effective resume is so specific, it's not easily transferable. Having to learn and improve these skills can lead to feeling resentful because you're wasting your time, and frustration at knowing how important it is, yet not having the ability to produce a quality product.

- There is good news. Pretty much *everything* involved at *every* step of the process is a skill, and as such *can* be developed and honed, and you can get better. Some of the skills *are* transferable, useful and worthwhile enough in their own right to spend time and effort to develop. I'll tell you which ones, so you don't waste your time.

2. **It's all about them, not you — you need to use your empathy**

    I really thought the whole process was about me – I needed a job, I have great communication skills, I have managed team conflict in a previous position – let me tell you what I think you should know about me! Now, while you do have to 'sell' yourself, and be able to write and talk about your skills, experience and knowledge, I want you to turn this around using your empathy – walk a few steps in someone else's shoes.

    You getting a job is actually all about the recruiter – the person or people doing the recruitment – and to make it even more difficult, 'the recruiter' may be a number of different people.

    Firstly, the person listed as the contact for the position, then the person(s) who will review your resume, cover letter and selection criteria, next the person(s) who will interview you, and finally the person(s) who will make the actual hire decision. For example,

    - In a project management position I applied for, I initially applied to a recruitment agent. I managed to sneak past them, and my resume was passed to the Human Resources Manager for the organization.
    - This person did an initial vetting of applications and cull, and then passed these applications to the manager of the position, who decided who to interview from the smaller set.

STEP 1 - Prepare yourself to think differently

- Once selected for an interview, I faced a panel made up of the manager, another department manager from within the organization, and an external person from the sector.
- The manager and CEO made the final hiring decision, and I happily accepted the project.

> Each stage of the recruitment process has a different aim, and the person involved at each stage may think differently, have different perspectives and time constraints, have varying motivation and influence over the hiring decision and unpredictable levels of skill and depth of experience in recruitment.

Later in this chapter you'll learn that at every step of the process, you can use some simple cognitive reappraisal techniques (a way of framing your mind) to assist you, and in this instance, specifically repositioning. Repositioning, as you'll discover, is seeing a situation from someone else's perspective.

I'll encourage you at various steps throughout the book to imagine yourself in the situation of the person at each stage of the process and consider carefully what that means for how you tackle each task.

3. Getting a job is all about taking the long view

From a financial perspective at the time, I desperately needed a job because I was due to have a baby in five months. Without thinking, I took the pragmatic view of landing a short-term contract. And I jumped in with both feet and applied for any, and all, positions quite separately.

- In comparison, I now take the view that all the activities you are going to undertake to get a particular job are not isolated – they are not *just* about writing *this* application to land *this* job. If you look, you will see the potential future worth of everything you do, and all the time you commit.

- A simple example is writing selection criteria with a view to reusing them time and again for new applications and then even using them for a future performance appraisal, when you do have a job.

- Spend time and give focus to developing relationships with people doing recruitment, not with landing this job as your outcome, but with the relationship itself as an outcome. They may not give you *this* job but might well play a part in landing you a job in the future.

Spend time and give focus to developing relationships with people doing recruitment, not with landing this job as your outcome, but with the relationship itself as an outcome.

Getting a job is a numbers game

Fifty-five jobs with one job interview and no job to show for it, was a pretty long haul for me, with no reward at the end! However, I was working with the expectation that I would fix my resume up a bit, spend a couple of hours searching for jobs, write one application, and then I'd land that job.

I definitely did *not* take the long view, and it's completely understandable that I felt disappointed and depressed when I didn't get an interview, let alone a job.

Setting great expectations

I *expected* to land a job immediately. The more applications I did, and the further I got from my original expectation, the more distressed I became. If instead I had expected to write quite a

STEP 1 - Prepare yourself to think differently

few applications, only score a couple of interviews, and then finally land one of those jobs, I would not have been affected as dramatically when I failed to land a job immediately.

> " *Expectations are about changing your perception.* "

Expectations are about changing your perception. David Rock in his book *Your Brain at Work,* asserts that if you are able to keep your expectations low, and avoid unmet expectations, then you will minimize the threat response (a physiological reaction to a perceived harmful event) in your brain which cause emotions such as anxiety, sadness and fear.

Mike's Story

A coaching client of mine, Mike, was an insurance salesman of the old kind. Mike had cut his teeth walking the streets going door-to-door selling insurance. He built his successful business through effective sales techniques and maintained that his sales ratio was 100 people marketed to would roughly result in 10 sales meetings, which would then in turn result in one sale.

And while getting a job is not exactly sales, and this is not the actual ratio, I have found this a useful baseline expectation to have while searching for a job. For each 100 jobs you apply for, you can expect around 10 interviews and that will land you the one job you're looking for.

Now, I know this sounds a bit crazy, but don't panic!

I don't think you're going to have to write 100 job applications to land your job. This numbers game concept is about setting your expectations.

Anthony's story

In reality, the people I've worked with don't come anywhere close to writing 100 applications. The closest I've seen to the actual numbers was Anthony, a man in his mid-50s who I coached when he was made redundant.

Having spent a long time in retail, Anthony was now trying to get a manual job (gardening, handyman, driving). He had the huge obstacle of a worker's compensation claim for a now-recurring injury affecting his work. A tough ask, right?

Well, his score was 87 applications (over an eight-month period), which resulted in 12 interviews until he landed his job. He *did* trust the process, he *did* persist, and as a result he *did* land a job.

The best news is, you are, even now, working actively on managing your expectations. The best way to manage your expectations is to pay attention to them. Having just read this section you will already be thinking about where your expectations lie in regard to landing a job, and how much work you will have to put in.

> *The best way to manage your expectations is to pay attention to them.*

Putting aside my big three mistakes, I did do at least one thing right!

I did think effectively about how I approached the *task* of getting a job. As I was no longer working, I treated this task as if it was my job. The fact that I didn't get a job wasn't through lack of trying on my part.

STEP 1 - Prepare yourself to think differently

Getting a job is now your job

I looked at the job of getting a new job, as my job – I believed this, and felt the energy behind that belief. And this was particularly relevant as I wasn't working. If you're desperate to move from the job you are currently at or you're not working now, you need to think and act at all times as if:

Your current job is getting a job

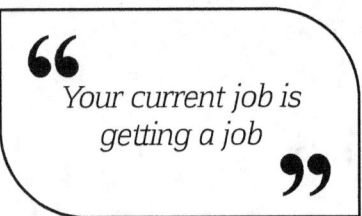
Your current job is getting a job

However, unlike what I did, this is not just about spending the time you would normally be at work, doing job-search activities. It's also about how you might act and what you might do in a job.

You want to be good at your job, succeed at what you're doing, right?

When you are in a job you find out what you're supposed to do, you do it the best way you can and try to get better at doing it, while achieving the targets you're measured against.

In the same way, if 'getting a job' is your job, you will want to understand what you need to do, try to get better at doing it, and achieve your targets. I'm going to help you every step of the way, but this is *your* job.

This shift in thinking helps directly with your motivation (and later your persistence). If you look at this as your 'main' job, you can apply different personal motivators for when things get tough, or if you are rejected for a job, or you find it hard to apply some of the new skills.

It can help with your priorities and your effort level – if this is your job, then you have an obligation to set goals and prioritize achieving them, and the efforts you put in to achieve these goals will potentially be higher.

How to think differently

In my recovery after the soul-destroying months of job applications, I did start to think about things differently, but this was not a simple process for me. It took a lot to convince myself of the importance of thinking differently, and just because I might say something to myself, didn't mean I actually believed it.

Since then, and with the benefit of working with others to change their thinking, I've discovered some science that helps. The following theory based on neuroscience is worthwhile talking about here because it underpins a lot of what we'll talk about in the rest of the book.

Cognitive Reappraisal

There's a psychological strategy called cognitive reappraisal (or just reappraisal). It sounds impressive but it's simply the concept of choosing to see a situation, or the meaning of a situation, in a different way in order to change the impact it has on you emotionally.

The benefits of controlling your interpretation of a situation can assist in changing the (negative) feelings associated at different places in the job searching process. And you may not realize it yet, but this may be a significant part of your difficulties – it certainly was for me.

> *There's a psychological strategy called cognitive reappraisal (or just reappraisal). It sounds impressive but it's simply the concept of choosing to see a situation, or the meaning of a situation, in a different way in order to change the impact it has on you emotionally.*

In his book *Your Brain at Work*, David Rock sets out four main types of reappraisal: reinterpreting, normalizing, reordering and repositioning. In order to change your thinking, you will have the opportunity to use them all.

Cognitive Reappraisal Types	
1. Reinterpreting	Reinterpreting an event is where you decide a threatening event is no longer a threat. It's quite common for people to view a job interview as a threatening event… well, at least not a pleasant one! Later in the book in Step 6, you will work diligently to reach a point where you can enjoy job interviews. Trust me. If you can reinterpret interviews as non-threatening and look forward to them, you will feel less stress, and will consequently perform better.
2. Normalizing	Normalizing is a common technique that takes what you believe to be abnormal and acknowledges it as normal. For example, being able to acknowledge that feeling anger and frustration during the job search process is completely normal. By doing this you feel more in control of, and able to let go of, things that are mostly out of your control.
3. Reordering	Reordering *information* is exactly as it sounds, reordering things in your brain. For example, in your job search process, I will work with you to reorder the value of each step of the process. At the moment, you most likely believe the aim of submitting a written application is to land a job. I will challenge that belief and ask you to reorder it in your brain, so you can see the value of a written application is just to land an interview.

4. Repositioning	Repositioning is described as changing the context through which you see a situation. You will implement repositioning at almost every step of the way in your new job/career search and you'll do this by taking the perspective of the person doing the recruitment. I will 'drill' you to stop thinking so much about *you* at each step and reposition how you think about the step, in terms of the person doing the recruitment. This was all I did to land the first job I applied for after maternity leave, the one that was the first step in my new career. If you do nothing else in this book except effectively implement the concept of repositioning, the chances of you landing your new job or career are going to dramatically increase.

I will come back to these concepts throughout the book. You will use them again and again to think differently and do things differently. But right now, thinking differently is just the start.

Now it's time to get clarity on what it is you actually want from this process, and this is where we're heading in the next step.

Don't worry if you feel like I'm moving slowly at the moment, or that this is taking too much time, and you haven't *done* anything yet. Now that you're thinking about reinterpreting, normalizing, reordering and repositioning your approach to your new job or career, that's all about to change.

To start the ball rolling, let me normalize this for you, and say that your impatience and possible frustration is completely normal. What I hope you're willing to do is trust me. I've learned the very hard way; you don't have to.

Spending a little time now, helps you avoid wasting time later and will mean you achieve the result you want faster in the end.

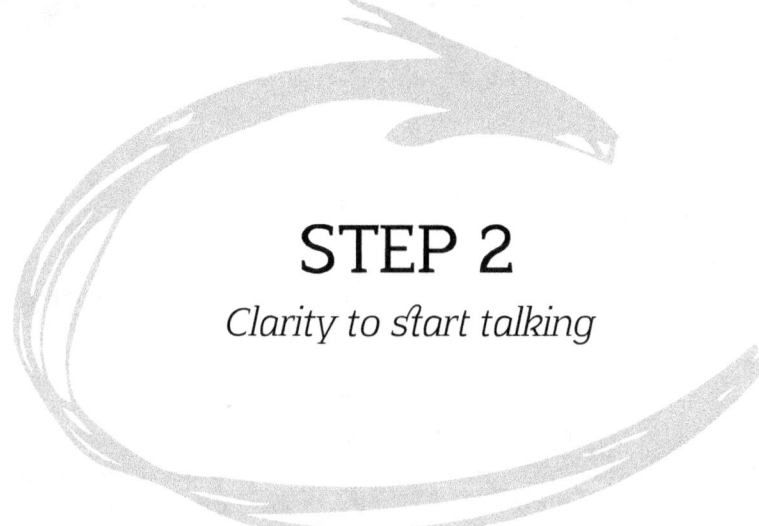

STEP 2
Clarity to start talking

You don't know what you don't know, till you know it

I didn't know that I actually wanted a whole new career at the time of my 55 job applications. I did have some inkling that I wasn't happy in Information Technology, but because I lost my job unexpectedly, I short-circuited any reflection time on my happiness or my career, and went straight into solution-mode. My solution at the time was to look for a different role in the same field, that might satisfy me and my short-term requirements.

It was only when it didn't go as planned, and I stepped away from everything completely, that things began to percolate differently, and I had space to reflect on them.

Annie's story

Contrast my experience with Annie who came to work with me, not unhappy in her job as a social worker, but not happy either. There had been much organizational change at her work recently and the answer to whether she should leave her current job went from yes to no to yes, depending on the day.

As a sole parent, Annie had financial responsibilities, she was the sole earner, and this weighed heavily on her mind whenever the leave/don't leave question raised its head. She first came to our coaching on a 'yes' day, when she felt she needed assistance to draft her resume so she could leave the current job. In this session, we worked through the *Drop-Dead List* exercise that I'll ask you to do in a minute. This list helps to get clarity on what you want and don't want in your career or new job *OR* get your conscious and subconscious minds thinking about what your next step might be. After we did this with Annie, she left with accountability tasks to complete before our next session. She was to reflect more on her *Drop-Dead List*, and to apply for two new positions for social work that had been advertised.

On returning for her second session, Annie excitedly announced, "I totally surprised myself! I enrolled to study Creative Writing at University."

To my surprise, Annie had also submitted one of her short stories to a competition. When reflecting on her *Drop-Dead List* she realized that she loved writing fiction and had done this as a hobby in her spare time. So it had 'popped into her head' that she should study creative writing.

In the short month since her first session, Annie had also completed her other tasks. She had applied for both new roles and had received an interview for one of them. She told me then that the interview had gone well but was unsure whether the role was for her.

At the third coaching session, Annie advised me that she'd won the writing competition and a small cash prize, but had not won the new job. But the surprising thing for her was that she was not disappointed at all. During that third session, she became decisively clear.

Annie made a decision to stay in her current job, but social work was no longer the career she wanted to pursue. She would now study at university and support herself with her current job, while forming her new career in writing.

Although her work still has up and down days, Annie *feels* completely different about staying in the job for the purpose of supporting herself financially while actively doing those things needed for her new career.

There is so much in what Annie has done to get to this point

1. All her decisions stemmed from the *Drop-Dead List* exercise, which she actively entered into, fully reflecting on what she had, and didn't have, and what she really wanted.

2. She took up my invitation to stay open to possibilities outside her original question of 'should I stay in this job or get a new one?' And to expect insights to come to her when she was least expecting it. David Rock in *Your Brain at Work* talks about the 'insight experience' which is a sudden 'knowing' of an answer to a problem, rather than a logical progression to get to the answer.

   You can expect these 'sudden revelations' to come at the most unusual times and places, for example, in the shower or while going for a walk. This is your subconscious brain solving the problem.

3. Annie made a conscious decision to stay in her current job and got clarity on *why* she would stay. This is light years away from staying in a job because you haven't made the decision to leave (or stay), or you haven't done the hard thinking, and pushed yourself to make a decision.

This decision making is important for a number of reasons. It gives you certainty; in Annie's case she has decided to stay at her current job and is no longer experiencing the stress of feeling in limbo. She now has a feeling of being more in control. From David Rock's book *Your Brain at Work*, he asserts *choosing* to experience stress is less stressful than experiencing stress without a sense of choice or control. Recognizing you have choices makes stress feel more manageable. Staying at your current job can be a valid choice, if you choose it.

Understanding what you want and need

So, let's work from the premise that right now you think you need a new job or a new career. I invite you to be open to the possibility that your next step, the end outcome of this process, may not in fact be a new job, or a new career. It may or may not be what you think. I have found, more times than you would imagine, that people start out thinking they are unhappy in their current job, and want to move to a new one, but end up somewhere completely different.

> *Recognizing you have choices makes stress feel more manageable.*

Remember Mike, the insurance salesman? At first, when he started coaching with me, he wanted to look at ways to expand his financial advisory business. However, his aim during coaching changed to setting up his succession plan for the business and moving to semi-retirement!

Articulating your Wants and Needs

I have already mentioned the importance of setting expectations, so now let me set some for the *Drop-Dead List* exercise.

This exercise asks you to think and reflect on what you're good at, what you like and don't like in your current job, and what you would *really* like in your new one.

Quite often what pops out as an insight during the process, is something completely different and unexpected. So, don't be surprised if it turns out that:

- ▶ What you really want, or need is not a job
- ▶ Or not a job in the form you thought you originally wanted
- ▶ Or it's not that new career you've been thinking about
- ▶ Or perhaps it is, and now you have clarity about… whatever it is

Be open to the possibilities and don't be worried if any of this happens, the *Drop-Dead List* has enormous potential to help you find clarity and make decisions.

Learning about Yourself

The *Drop-Dead List* exercise not only assists you to understand and articulate what you want and need from a new job or a different career, it also addresses the final piece of the puzzle for achieving clarity – knowing more about yourself.

It helps you clarify:

- ▶ What are you good or not good at
- ▶ What you enjoy and do not enjoy

This is essential for moving on in the job search process. At each stage of the job application stage, you will try your hardest to 'sell' your skills, knowledge, experience and attitudes, so the potential interviewer 'buys' you, and chooses you for that job.

> **"**
> *To talk about yourself to others, you need to know yourself.*
> **"**

To *talk* about yourself to others, you need to *know* yourself. The good news is that 'knowing yourself' is just information that can be collected and assimilated and retained. Let's focus now on the knowing (so that you can search more effectively for jobs) – the skill of communicating this effectively in writing and verbally to others we'll deal with later (when applying for jobs).

The *Drop-Dead List* EXERCISE

The *Drop-Dead List* exercise asks you to consider and record the things you **want or need** in a job or career and also **what you don't want**.

Drop-Dead is for those things you cannot, or will not, compromise on. For example, you may need to earn a certain amount of money to keep your household running. This is a practicality of your life situation that needs to be taken into account, so your *Drop-Dead* income amount is $X and if a job or career choice can't achieve that, the job for you just drops dead.

The Drop-Dead List Steps

(after you understand the steps, you'll find a Drop-Dead List Chart to complete next)

Step 1	Find at least 30 minutes and a quiet space or put on some music. Do this exercise in an environment that helps you concentrate and think – you need to take your time and to focus on doing this and only this.
Step 2	Grab your *Drop-Dead List* questions and consider each one carefully. a. What are your *Drop-Dead*, simply must have's (if you don't have them, the job 'drops dead')? b. What would be nice to have? Don't be afraid to put your full wish list out there. c. What do you NOT want? d. Don't be scared or think something is silly and not put it down. It doesn't matter how small or insignificant something may seem, or how unachievable, just record everything for now.
Step 3	Don't just read the questions and consider your responses. It's important to record your answers to each question as you will return to the answers again over the next few days, so consider how you record your answers. You may choose to type into a document, you might write freehand and use pencils or different colored pens, or you might speak into a voice recorder and talk it through for yourself. The main thing is, you can come back to your answers later — the way you record your answers only makes a difference to you, and how you best learn and process.

STEP 2 - Clarity to start talking

Step 4	If you get stuck – to normalize here for you – it's totally normal to get a bit stuck on one or more of these questions. If you get really stuck, and you need other input, here are a few ideas: a. Leave it and come back to it later, let it 'percolate' and see what comes to the surface b. Ask someone for help. It could be a work colleague or a family member or a friend, someone who knows you well and will give you some honest feedback c. If you are truly blocked on the job related questions, rather than those about you, try skipping ahead to Step 3 in the book, and do the *Job Awareness Building* Exercise. Then come back to this step and continue on.
Step 5	When you've finished, put the list aside somewhere because you will come back to it later.
Step 6	Over the next few days, weeks or sometimes months, come back to the list a number of times and add, tweak or remove things, leaving time between for reflections to come through. Often, having started your brain thinking about these questions, your subconscious will deliver you something you didn't think about when first writing your answers or a valuable insight that hadn't occurred to you before.
Step 7	As you come back to the list each time, read aloud your answers. This is a really important step, so don't skip it because you feel a little foolish talking to yourself!

Step 8	When you think you've spent enough time considering and answering the questions, left enough time for things to pop up, or you feel it's finished (for now), find someone to talk this through with. It doesn't have to be anyone specific; the idea is to articulate your thoughts to someone else. It could be a family member, friend, colleague or a coach if you have one. Again, there is science behind this too, as David Rock says in his book *Your Brain at Work*, "When you speak to someone about something, more parts of your brain are activated than when you just think about it, and this makes it easier to recall ideas later on." David also contends other people aren't locked into your way of thinking about a problem, so often others may have an insight you can't access yourself.

Following the *Drop-Dead List* exercise, you will undoubtedly have clarity about your direction. You will finally be ready to *do* something! However, rather than looking for a job, you might find yourself with another set of accountability tasks altogether. For example, you might want to look into further study like Annie.

If so, off you go and come back to the book when you need a new job in the future. If not, and you have clarity about the direction of the job you're looking for, let's start looking for jobs that fit what you want and need on your *Drop-Dead List*, those jobs that now fit your new understanding of yourself.

STEP 2 - Clarity to start talking

Drop-Dead List

You can download a blank Drop-Dead List Chart for free at www.whatnowcareer.com/resources

What is really important to you? What are your values? What rules do you live by? (Include those you just can't work with, for example if honesty is important to you, you might write that you will not work with dishonest people.)		
What is your idea of the perfect job? Be expansive and detailed in your thinking, e.g. *A job where I work in a close group of about five people, both men and women – I like them as people, and they make me laugh. We are working on something I feel is really important and the others share that sense of importance. We are working on something exciting, that has an 'end', like an event or a project. There is nice, healthy food to eat for lunch somewhere nearby. I have to do some writing, but not a huge amount, and I don't have to do any numbers or working with figures. I feel I can rely on the team, and they rely on me. I am my own boss and I am free to create my own tasks and deliver as I see fit. People look to me for assistance and advice. If I have a 'boss', this relationship feels like we are peers.*		
What are your 'deal-breaker' requirements? - $ - Travel distance/time - Travel type - Level of work - Type of work (what industry, what kind of job, part-time/full-time) - Conditions – leave, flexibility, etc - Any restraints or constraints (e.g. physical limitations) - Work alone/in a team/both - What else?	**DROP DEAD LIST** *(need)*	**WISH LIST** *(want)*

What is your wish list for things you *wish* you could have in a job?

What are you good at?

Now, what are you *REALLY* good at? (This does NOT have to relate to jobs or work, think about you in your whole life. Although they may be on your list, for example cooking or basketball, a more personal example might be, 'I am <u>really</u> good at paying attention to children, making them feel heard and then surprising them with something they don't expect to hear from an adult.')

What do you like doing?

What did you enjoy spending time doing as a child?

When do you feel/have you felt 'in the flow'? When do you completely lose track of time while doing something? (Again, not necessarily in a work situation, could be while knitting!)

STEP 2 - Clarity to start talking

What do you really not want to do? What fills you with dread?
(e.g. Working on my own in a room with no windows. Having to work on my own. Having a micro manager as a boss. No flexibility in terms of when and how I work.)

When you have had a *really* good day at work, describe how you are and how you feel when you get home at the end of the day. (e.g. I collapse, physically exhausted into a chair and my brain is buzzing and feels a little fried because I have been using it all day. I feel contented and I go over in my head something nice someone said to me, and also a comment someone who I respect made to me about the good work I was doing. I feel satisfied with how what I did turned out today and feel excited thinking about tomorrow when I go back!)

Think of a time at work (volunteer or paid) where you were most happy? What was it about that time that made you happy? (e.g. I was doing things that pushed me out of my comfort zone, but not too far, I loved the people I was working with, I had fun and laughed properly, many times every day)

What else haven't you said about jobs/careers above? Include both the good and the bad! (I don't deal well with incompetence especially in leadership or I love working with a well-run and handled team)

NOW, tell me about what you want in a job/new career. What are the *really* important parts of your answers that stand out to you?

STEP 3

*Seek and Search –
The numbers game*

New-found clarity on your overall direction may get you excited to start job searching, but you might not be effective in that pursuit as yet, and that's exactly what happened with Paul, a very action-driven client of mine.

Paul's story

Paul was determined to leave his current job when he came to me, wanting a complete change in career.
After completing his *Drop-Dead List*, he had the surprising insight that he loved his actual job (practice manager for a chain of for-profit childcare centers), but wanted to move to the non-profit community services sector to use his skills and experience to help others in a meaningful way.

He was excited by this realization, and immediately started searching for practice manager positions in community services. The only one (big) issue was that this job wasn't called a 'Practice Manager' in his new target industry.

STEP 3 - Seek and Search – The numbers game

During his early searching, he missed out on the equivalent jobs because they were commonly referred to as 'Operations Manager' and 'Chief Operating Officer' positions. He simply didn't know they existed and were equivalent. With his searches not yielding many jobs to apply for, he came back for additional assistance, and then spent time doing the *Job Awareness Building (JAB)* exercise (below).

This resulted in him widening his search of positions and landing his dream job as Chief Operating Officer with a large community services agency.

———————————————————————

The JAB Exercise: Job Awareness Building

If you have no idea what you might be interested in in terms of a new career, or if you are new to, or re-entering the workforce following a break, or you are struggling to answer questions in the *Drop-Dead List* exercise in Step 2, then the good news is that this exercise can help.

Open yourself to the potential connectedness of seemingly unrelated information in this process. You can collect all sorts of information about the current job market that may prove surprisingly useful to you as you continue your job seeking.

	Job Awareness Building Steps
Step 1	Decide on a popular and general job search website (see **Searching advertised jobs** section below for some examples). Don't choose a specialized job search website, but one that advertises all industries and types of work.
Step 1	Set yourself an accountability task to set aside time to research and regularly browse job ads on this website, with a minimum of five separate sessions (about an hour per session). You might commit to searching for these jobs for 45 minutes each day for a week, or three days one week and three days the next week, one hour per session. Do more if you think you need it.
Step 3	When you get to your allocated time, do a search on any location and All Sectors of jobs – anything from a mechanic to a molecular biologist with all types of employment (for example, contract and permanent positions). We're doing this as an awareness building exercise, so the further the jobs are away from what you currently do, or are interested in doing, the better. This may give you different ideas as they are outside your current sphere of knowledge.
Step 4	Spend your allotted time browsing through the job advertisements, opening and reading any available position descriptions.

STEP 3 - Seek and Search – The numbers game

Step 5	Jot down notes as you go of anything that catches your interest or curiosity and items you react strongly to, regardless of whether it's a positive or negative reaction. Ignore the qualifications or requirements. For example, you might look at a Winery Manager advertisement, knowing nothing about grapes or wine! Ignore the need for a university degree in viticulture, instead have a look at what the job entails and what they're offering. You might read the ad and be interested that it involves working outside tending to vines. You might also react negatively to the requirement to work three weekends out of four. Record these things and any insights you gain from them. A simple table for you to keep track and keep adding to each session, might look like this. You can download a blank Job Awareness Building Worksheet for free at www.whatnowcareer.com/resources	
What caught my interest?	**What do I *think* or *feel* about this?**	**What this might mean for my next job/career is…** **The insight for me is….**
"You will work weekends, with every fourth weekend off."	*That is a lot to work both days of each weekend and only have 1 in 4 off. I won't be able to spend weekend time with kids very often.*	*Weekend work is okay, would prefer just Saturday work rather than whole weekend, or maximum 1 on 1 off weekend*

	"Fancy a job where you don't have to sit in an office all the time?"	Fantastic! I feel really excited!	Working outside for most of my time at work would be fabulous. Also, I don't want to be stuck in an office 5 days a week 9-5.
Step 6		Do manual searches, and don't set alerts or email delivery for jobs. You are hunting – hunting for jobs, hunting for things of interest to you, and going where your interest takes you, rather than a static search for a narrow set of jobs. This searching is proactive, rather than reacting to things delivered to you, with the added benefit that you feel a bit more in control of the whole process.	
Step 7		After repeating your searching numerous times, you may well start to see a pattern, or patterns, emerging – details will start to stand out that didn't before, and it will be the same sorts of things over and over. Using our Winery Manager example, you might find you've recorded a number of jobs involving outside work and gain the insight that you would find an outside job attractive.	
Step 8		Once patterns have emerged, now what? Firstly, use this information to further refine your *Drop-Dead List*. It's all about developing your awareness further: what you want, what you don't want, what you would like or love to have in your next job.	

The beautiful thing about this awareness is, you don't need to do anything specific as far as your brain is concerned. Just by paying attention to them, by bringing these out of your subconscious into your consciousness, you will now be more attuned to seeing and finding these aspects in your job searches. This is known as the *Baader-Meinhof phenomenon*, where your brain gets excited by the fact you've learned something new, and selective attention occurs. Your brain looks for this new thing without you realizing it, and you start to see it everywhere.

The more information you have to start to build your search for a job, even if it's seemingly peripheral information, the greater the likelihood of something popping out at you as you go.

The easiest way to find and land a job

Once you have developed a broadened self-awareness of what you want and need, and what is available in the job market, and perhaps had a breakthrough moment where you've realized what you really want to do, it's time to find and land those jobs.

The easiest way to land a job is for someone to offer you one

Someone who knows you and likes you or knows you in a work situation and works well with you, and also knows you want a job. Seriously, I've seen this happen many times – 'it's not what you know, it's who you know' at its finest.

Rachelle's story

Rachelle is a prime example. She left school at 15 and had a varied work career in administration, then quit in her late 20s to take care of her baby. When her baby was 18 months old, she separated from her husband and found herself a single mother who had to return to work to support herself and her baby. She started a new career as a children's swim school instructor, which was reasonable in terms of bringing in money and excellent for the flexibility to care for her daughter. As a bonus, she loved swimming and spending time in the water.

Rachelle continued in this career contentedly for a number of years, eventually starting to think of ways to further this career as she had moved into swim center management.

When I began coaching Rachelle, it was to start her own swim school. This, she thought, would give her stability, building an asset for herself and her daughter for the future. She happily continued with this idea, drawing up plans for building alterations to house a pool and even buying the pool.

At around the same time, Rachelle started having trouble with her skin due to chlorine. She was becoming despondent that she may no longer be able to work as a swim instructor (which made the proposition of running a profitable swim school harder).

So, now what?

In coaching, Rachelle worked through her *Drop-Dead List* and identified her important things:

1. Flexibility to take care of her daughter

2. Better money

3. Somewhere not in an environment with chlorine

4. Job stability

I also had Rachelle do an exercise to consider her network of friends and family, and she courageously reached out to many of them, telling them she was on the lookout for a new career. One of these friends worked for a government department and although her friend was supportive of her request, they also had a good giggle at the thought that Rachelle would ever qualify for the kind of role that her friend had. Within three months, this friend contacted Rachelle advising a casual job was going in another program that might be suitable. Although being completely different to anything Rachelle had ever done before, and definitely something she thought was out of her reach due to lack

STEP 3 - Seek and Search – The numbers game

of a tertiary education, it fitted ALL her *Drop-Dead List* requirements.

Coaching then turned to applying effectively for this role, completely reworking her resume, and overcoming her limiting belief that she was not adequately educated for this role. The happy ending for Rachelle is she has now been a permanent full-time public servant for over 10 years and has worked her way up through the ranks and a variety of positions, to pre-executive level.

Although Rachelle did absolutely no 'hard' work job searching to land her job, she did a lot of 'smart' work to get there – she worked smarter, not harder!

>
> *Although Rachelle did absolutely no 'hard' work job searching to land her job, she did a lot of 'smart' work to get there – she worked smarter, not harder!*
>

You can use her lessons to help you land your job, by:

1. Openly reflecting on what you want, and realistically considering your needs through the *Drop-Dead List*. Don't limit this thinking to what you have done previously or are doing currently.

2. Spend time articulating your wants and needs to people, making them real and tangible.

3. Employ courage to start having conversations with people you know, making it clear you are looking for work, and asking if anything comes up they think would be suitable, could they remember you.

4. Don't dismiss jobs due to limiting beliefs. Instead work through these beliefs, and then work hard on the written application, show how your skills and experience fit with this new and different position.

You can also use your empathy, and you can reposition your thinking. Walk for a brief minute in the shoes of the people in your network you might talk to – they care about you, and like you, they would be pleased to be able to help you out, and what's more, you might actually be doing them a favor!

Imagine a job becomes available in their team after talking with you. They know they like you, know your capabilities in terms of work, and they can just offer you the job. Compare this to writing a job ad, culling written applications, running a day of interviews and then still potentially selecting someone who doesn't turn out perfectly for the position.

Which one do you think will make their life easier? Which one will they happily choose if they can?

How do you let people know you are on the lookout for work?

You can *ask* them if they have anything available, and you can *tell* them you are looking for work! If you are not comfortable with this idea, it helps to write and practice saying, a simple script for how to approach them. Get started with these ones, and tailor to your situation and the person you approach:

- ▶ Do you have a job going for me?
- ▶ You work for XYZ company don't you? I would be really interested in working for them. Do you know if they have any positions available at the moment?
- ▶ I'm keen to move on from my current job and I know you love your job. How would I go about finding out when positions become available at your work?

STEP 3 - Seek and Search – The numbers game

> ► You know I need to move on from my current job. I'd really appreciate if you hear of something to keep me in mind, or let me know so that I can apply.

Another easy way to find and land a job – Volunteering

Volunteering is especially useful if you are thinking of changing careers. Think of it in terms of 'try before you buy' – volunteering time working in the new industry or career to check it meets your *Drop-Dead List*.

The bonus is, quite often unpaid work can lead to paid work, either through a direct offer to come on as paid staff, or indirectly as you are now an 'insider'.

And there are other significant benefits of volunteering. You will be able to gather information relevant to this job/career that you can use to give you an edge when applying for paid positions. You can also add to your resume some direct, relevant and current work experience in the industry you are seeking to enter, and fill any gaps in employment on your resume. It may even afford you a valuable opportunity to acquire new skills and grow your networks, and provide a critical sense of purpose at a time when you sorely need it.

Win-win all round, I reckon!

Nancy's story

Nancy was a client of mine who experienced a win this way. She had worked hard for over 20 years as an auditor and was completely worn out. She took a self-funded career break to have some downtime to find a new career and came to me for coaching.

Nancy was quite clear she wanted to move from what she saw as 'clinical' auditing and accounting and helping the 'bottom line' of companies, to helping people. Other than that, she had no idea!

Over the next three months, Nancy attended a number of places to volunteer: training as a volunteer counsellor, assisting at a veterinary surgery, working with young children at a childcare center, and spending time with the elderly at an aged care facility.

She quickly ruled the first three out, but found she enjoyed working with the elderly, and so started looking into qualifications for working in aged care. During this time, Nancy also did her Drop-Dead List and her JAB exercise, and used them as live documents, revisiting these as she gathered new information about herself and what she wanted.

Nancy also talked with some of her network working in community service agencies letting them know she was changing careers. A work colleague from over 10 years ago, who enjoyed working with Nancy and knew her work, called her to offer her a short-term volunteer project position, where she would have an opportunity to work in a small organization providing disability services to children.

While it was an administration project, Nancy accepted it to have a firsthand look at the work they undertook with children. During this short project, the organization fell in love with Nancy, and she similarly fell in love with the organization.

Following this experience, Nancy reflected that what she had found was different to what she had been searching for. She found a small team where it felt like family, and a purposeful reason for the work they had her doing. The kind of work she was carrying out didn't matter.

Nancy was offered a full-time role as a project officer for this organization after a few short-term projects, and she is now happily working in her new setting, and the organization is over the moon with their highly qualified and motivated project officer.

Looking for volunteer opportunities

To find a volunteer opportunity, follow the guidelines for searching for paid work opportunities later in this chapter, keeping in mind there are dedicated volunteering job websites where volunteer positions are advertised which are excellent sources.

Searching for jobs that don't exist

This might sound weird, but this is as simple (and as hard) as identifying organizations you might like to work for and approaching them. This is a commonly recommended method of finding and landing a job, but seldom taken up – the main reason being the perception it will be a lot of work for potentially no reward (as a job doesn't exist)!

Alessandro's story

Alessandro, a young client of mine, didn't let this get in his way to find and land his dream job. He had finished school a year previously and had chosen not to do further study. He was quite content working casual hours at a local theme park, but wanted to move out of home, so his motivation became finding find a job to support this. Starting as always at the beginning, he put together his Drop-Dead List and almost immediately had a realization that he had a dream job, but didn't think it was a viable one.

Alessandro was a night-owl and didn't like some of the early starts he had with his current job, but he loved the playful interactions he had with customers at the theme park. He had inherited an appreciation and in-depth knowledge of gin (the liquor) from his father and he decided being a bartender in a city gin bar would be his dream job. So, now what!?

Now to find a job as a bartender in a gin bar in the city! Unfortunately, they don't tend to advertise on websites, and most of these rare positions would be filled by word of mouth. Alessandro didn't know any gin bar owners or bartenders so his first accountability task was to research city gin bars and then narrow this list down to those he might like to work for.

I then had him do an exercise to walk a minute in the shoes of a manager of a bar, and what they might like to see in a bartender (what would their selection criteria be if they advertised a position?).

Alessandro decided they would want an excellent knowledge of gins, good customer service skills and most importantly a bit of personality. This required a complete revamp of his resume, which had been tailored as a school leaver looking for retail part-time work, and not with this job in mind.

STEP 3 - Seek and Search – The numbers game

Alessandro returned to me a resume with a bright red border and matching red headings. I assisted him to write a cover letter (which, by the way, matched the resume design-wise, with red colored accents throughout the letter). He wrote the cover letter addressing the criteria we had identified and specifically designed the letter to be handed (with the resume) to the bar manager/owner after Alessandro had walked in off the street and spoken to them for a few minutes about his passion to work in a gin bar.

He landed his dream job on the third bar he approached!

———————————————

I had Alessandro really think and act, outside the square for this one. And you can too:

1. Be open to completely radical ideas that pop out, seemingly from nowhere, from your Drop-Dead List. And have the courage to go with an idea, even if it's quite different from the jobs you think you should be applying for.
2. Put yourself in the shoes of the person hiring for the job you want, so that you can tailor your resume and cover letter.
3. Get motivated and put in loads of work up front, without any guarantee of payback – even if there is no advertised job.
4. Have the courage to circumvent the usual 'rules' of resume writing to present an incredibly tailored resume based on empathy for the potential employer.
5. And again, access your courage and enthusiasm to go door-to-door and approach people.

Searching advertised jobs

This is the last thing on your finding-jobs list. In this task you search for advertised jobs. You just need to find the ones you want to apply for. So, where to look?

1. Give some thought to where the jobs you might be interested in are advertised and do research if the answer is not clear. Not all jobs are advertised on job search websites. Some jobs (for example, wait staff in a café) are still commonly advertised by a sign in the front window

2. Local or regional locations often have a Facebook page for local jobs, so search and ask around on Facebook to see what might be available in your area

3. Popular job search websites. Refer to the following table for specific examples current at the writing of this book. Your search will include:

    a. LinkedIn
    b. General job search websites
    c. Specific industry/sector websites. For example, there are specific non-government organization (NGO) and particular industry websites, e.g. music, technology
    d. Government job search sites (for state/province and federal)
    e. Recruitment agencies

STEP 3 - Seek and Search – The numbers game

	Australia	USA	UK	Canada
General job search sites	SEEK https://www.seek.com.au/ Indeed https://au.indeed.com/	Monster https://www.monster.com/ Indeed https://www.indeed.com/q-USA-jobs.html	Reed https://www.reed.co.uk/ Indeed https://www.indeed.co.uk/	Canada Jobs https://www.canadajobs.com/ Indeed https://ca.indeed.com/
Specific sites (examples only - do a search for your niche, there could be a specific job site)	The Arts – Arts Hub https://www.artshub.com.au/ Not for profit community work – Ethical Jobs https://www.ethicaljobs.com.au/ Short term work – OneShift https://au.oneshiftjobs.com/	Technical jobs – https://www.dice.com/	NHS (National Health Service) https://www.jobs.nhs.uk/	Music industry - https://www.glassdoor.ca/Job/canada-music-industry-jobs-SRCH_IL.0,6_IN3_KO7,21.htm Wine industry - https://www.winebusiness.com/s/canada/classifieds/winejobs/
Government Jobs	Australian Public Service Jobs https://www.apsjobs.gov.au/; Australian Jobsearch https://jobsearch.gov.au/ (and search for Jobs and your state to find state government sites)	USA Government Jobs https://www.usajobs.gov/	UK Civil Service Jobs https://www.civilservicejobs.service.gov.uk/csr/index.cgi	Canadian Government Jobs https://www.canada.ca/en/services/jobs/opportunities.html

4. Freelancing work websites:
    a. Advertising short-term skilled work, for example Airtasker (Australia and the UK) https://www.airtasker.com/.
    These sites allow people to list jobs they want done, for example, design and build a website, a house removal or a garden clean-up
    b. Specialist websites that coordinate contracting work, for example, if you want a job doing transcription of audio and video files, Rev https://www.rev.com/
5. Other online websites
    a. Newspapers and classifieds sites often have an employment section, for example, Gumtree in Australia and the UK https://www.gumtree.com.au/ - https://www.gumtree.com/

Doing your Searching

With all the excellent work you have put in and insights you've had so far, you should now have some idea of *what* to look for, but remember, broaden your search as much as possible to start with.

Set yourself an accountability target around how much searching you do for jobs. It can become an obsession, and you may find yourself searching nonstop and not having time to apply for anything. Or you may not spend enough time looking for jobs, in all the different places you might be able to find them.

Again, resist the urge to set email alerts from a couple of websites. Go on the hunt and find that job you want – and land it!

Minimize Overwhelm

1. To minimize any overwhelm by looking at too many jobs, you might choose to narrow your search by some 'must haves' from your *Drop-Dead List*. For example, you might only be

STEP 3 - Seek and Search – The numbers game

looking for part-time work or work in a particular location, so might narrow your search with these criteria.

2. Look at ALL the jobs in your chosen field(s), regardless of whether you think you have all the skills and experience they want, and also gather jobs that are at your level, a little step below and ones that are above what you perceive as your level.

3. Do not self-cull too dramatically. Often submitting an effective application can get you past the most stringent selection criteria. Obviously, if you need a degree for a medical practitioner job and you don't have one, you will be able to rule out that job! But sometimes even things like university degrees, often listed as essential criteria, are not always obligatory if you write an effective application. Put the effort in and apply for it, even if you think it's a long shot.

Do I need to be 100% qualified?

If you think you can do the job... then put in an application.

Sheryl Sandberg, who wrote the book *Lean In: Women, Work, and the Will to Lead*, quotes an internal Hewlett-Packard report that showed women only apply for jobs if they think they meet 100% of requirements, whilst men apply if they think they meet 60 percent.

Tara Sophia Mohr, when writing for the Harvard Business Review (HBR), was interested in this finding and a common interpretation from this study that women were less confident than men. In her HBR article *'Why Women Don't Apply for Jobs Unless They're 100% Qualified'*, she surveyed 1,000 people to find the top reason for both men and women. She found that the most common reason by far was, "I didn't think they'd hire me since I didn't meet the qualifications, and I didn't want to waste my time and energy."

https://hbr.org/2014/08/why-women-dont-apply-for-jobs-unless-theyre-100-qualified

The moral of this research is to make sure you apply for roles when you don't meet all the criteria. Don't let this phase you, particularly women. If you think you can do the job, and can show someone that ability on paper, then put in an application.

In our next step, Step 4, I address resumes that stand out. It's all about perspective and rewriting your history. Let's create a great resume together.

STEP 4

*Your Resume –
Rewrite your history*

I can't tell you how awful my 55-job application resume was. I look at my old one from time to time, and while I can now stop myself from cringing, I still feel a tingle of embarrassment.

I didn't even know how bad it was until a friend asked me if they could have a look at it because they wanted to update their own. I hadn't needed to use it for some years in my consulting practice, so hadn't looked at it. But as I had now been coaching people in job searching skills for a few years, I confidently passed it on to her, presuming it would be good!

My friend, who was going for an academic job, thanked me for sending it through, but said she thought it was a bit long and detailed for what she needed (it was five pages), and that she could 'certainly hear me talking' in it!

Well, that feedback gave me a bit of a surprise – was it really five pages long, and why could she hear me talking in it?

So, I had a look at it. In the intervening years since I'd last updated it, my skill set in resume reviewing and writing had improved markedly, and I was shocked at what I saw! That resume never saw

STEP 4 - Your Resume – Rewrite your history

the light of day again, and I found a couple of good templates for my friend to use for her Curriculum Vitae (CV) which she needed for an academic role.

A quick word on the difference between a Resume and Curriculum Vitae's (CV's)

I had a resume and my friend needed a CV... These terms are often used interchangeably, but they are in fact quite different documents.

Resume

A resume is a brief summary (one or two pages) of a person's skills and experience and tailored to a position.

Curriculum Vitae

A CV is detailed, static (over a person's work life) and can be much longer than two pages.

Resumes are most commonly required (unless you want a job that specifically requires a CV, such as my friend seeking a new academic position), so that's what we'll talk about.

You will need a resume, or two...

Unless you happen to luck into a job (rather than land one), you're going to need a resume. And you're likely better served if you have more than one. Don't panic, once you've got one, others are easier and less time consuming to put together. And you may end up with a number of resumes, with little tweaks that create a new version for a particular position or industry.

A useful approach can be to create a master version and then tailor slightly for each job you apply for, working back from the advertisement to ensure you cover the key requirements, skills and experience for the job. Even if you just edit your positioning statement (your professional summary) up front to align with what the hiring organisation is seeking in order to have an impact and make it easy for the reader to put your resume in the 'yes' pile.

> **Remember Alessandro getting his dream job in a gin bar?**
>
> Alessandro is a great example of this as he now has two resumes, one standard resume geared toward retail jobs, and also his gin bar (creative) resume. During coaching, Alessandro identified other avenues to try to achieve his aim of moving out of home.
>
> The first was 'just a job' to bring some money in to achieve his goal, and he thought he might enjoy working as a waiter. For these jobs I advised him to use his 'retail' resume for any application. The other avenue was to try for an entry-level job in audio technical work, and for these I recommended his bartender application showcasing his creative side.
>
> He didn't have time to pursue these, as he got his dream job quickly, but he is now set up for the future if he should want to move on.

(Don't) Write your Resume

If you can possibly get out of it, don't write your resume. Unless you like writing, *and* a challenge, *and* want to develop these skills. If this is you, go right ahead, and I'll even give you some hints a bit later. Otherwise, if you know someone who can write effective resumes, ask for their help to write yours.

STEP 4 - Your Resume – Rewrite your history

If you don't know anyone, and you can afford to pay someone to write your resume, do it. Look at it as a wise investment to be able to confidently submit any job application with a current resume which reflects your work history and skills appropriately and effectively. This is even more important if you require a very specific resume, say if you are changing careers or industries, or looking to get into a sector which has specific and rigid recruitment guidelines, for example, government jobs.

Other benefits of not writing your resume include:

- Not expending the considerable energy needed to learn the skill of writing this kind of document and experiencing the frustration that invariably comes with it. Resume writing is a specific skill which you may only use a few times in your working life. You can save your energy for other job-getting jobs.

- The person you get to draft your resume (if they're doing a good job) will have a discussion with you to find out some additional information. They will want to know your skills and capabilities, and what you're good at, so they can see how to pitch the resume and draft a summary about you. This discussion potentially offers you 'free' coaching to start considering the questions in your *Drop-Dead List* (see Step 2). You can't help but gain a better awareness and understanding of yourself through the process.

Now, if you do choose to get a career or job coach or a resume writer to draft your resume for you, keep in mind you get what you pay for. If you pay a cut-rate price, you will most likely get a vanilla resume based off a template.

That template may not be a good one, but the one the writer

is familiar with and can put together with the least amount of energy and time. They will take your old resume and re-write it and won't take the time to get to know you to tailor the resume appropriately.

The Aim of your Resume

The aim of your resume is simple, and it's not to actually to get you a job. Of course, it should *help* get you a job but the *actual* aim, usually, is to get you an interview. That's all.

How do you stand out enough on paper so that someone wants to interview you?

To write an effective resume (or be happy with one written for you), you need to break the paradigm that it is all about you. It does outline your skills and experience, but it is not, in the dramatic sense, all about you. Instead it's all about the audience. Usually the people responsible for culling written applications to find the best people 'on paper' to invite into an interview, are the audience.

Let's walk a minute in their shoes and step through what happens when a resume is received and what each step then means for your resume:

1. They will open the resume and may start to browse it, or they may print it off on paper immediately without even glancing through it. Your resume MUST look tidy and neat and easy to read on the screen AND on paper.

2. When that person sits down to read your resume, you have no way to predict their mood, their time constraints or their personal preferences. They may be preoccupied with

something else while reading your resume – their phone could ring three times and the reading of your resume may span more than an hour! This may be the first resume they open with excitement and anticipation, or it may be the 102nd they have opened knowing they still have over 60 left to look through.

3. The person reading the resume and in charge of doing the initial cull of applications, may have little or no experience on what to look for in a resume, or they may be a seasoned recruitment agent and have reviewed thousands of them.

You need to aim for the lowest common denominator here, and by this I don't mean to insult the people who will read it, but always assume, and write for, the 'worst' scenario:

1. Their first read (and maybe the only one) will be done in less than two minutes, while they drain the last of their cup of coffee before running into a meeting they are now late for. Good formatting is essential, as is succinct and effective capturing of your work experience, with most recent and relevant information always at the top.

2. The person reading your resume is not particularly skilled at recruitment and has limited capacity to pick up the potential of the person behind the paper. For example, if you are going for a job in a call centre, and the ad advises a high volume of calls, don't assume they will know the job you currently have (and recorded in your resume) as a Call Centre Operator has a high volume of calls – instead specify you receive a high volume of calls when describing your current employment. Even better put some actual numbers to define high volume so there is no doubt in their mind.

3. They will have already received a number of resumes and will be concerned about the time this process is taking.

4. Whatever is happening for them, at first they will most likely skim the resume, rather than read it, and so you need to stand out in some (good) way while they skim. A way to do this is with an authentic professional summary (positioning statement) right at the top. Follow this with the most relevant and well-crafted work experience summary. This again makes their job easier in finding what they are looking for quickly and easily.

So, the questions to ponder when composing a resume are NOT:

- ▶ What do *I* want to put in my resume or
- ▶ What do *I* want to tell people *I've* done or what skills *I* have

They become:

- ▶ What does the person potentially reading or skimming my resume want or need to see?
- ▶ What are *they* looking for?
- ▶ What's most important to *them*?
- ▶ How do I make this stand out quickly and with little effort for *them*?

STEP 4 - Your Resume – Rewrite your history

Owen's story

I consulted with Owen, a financial services client, to assist with the recruitment of a personal assistant. Both he and I thought this job would attract a lot of attention due to flexible work hours and being in an area with many people looking for local work, rather than face long commutes to the city.

We were still caught off guard when we received 147 applications in the first 18 hours of the job being advertised and closed the call for applications immediately (less than 24 hours after it had been posted online).

Having written the job advertisement which asked applicants to respond to provided selection criteria, the first cull I undertook was not to review any application that had not done this. I was left with over a hundred applications to consider.

Owen then made the next culling decision to discard applications without a university degree and thirty remained following this. I reviewed each individual resume, and it was clear that an expertly crafted resume, outlining their work experience and skills, set the applicant apart and would get them an interview. For example, one resume said 'Receptionist' as the job title (and assumed I, the culler, knew the details of that job), while another outlined the phone system used, how many calls they took on average and other duties they undertook while not answering phones.

The first was all guess work for me, and I would have to assume my idea of receptionist was the same as the applicants while the second gave me information that I could easily match to the job at hand.

I set up eight interviews from the 147 applications and Owen conducted the interviews. Interestingly, the person I selected as the 'front runner' after reading applications was offered the job by the client. Her 'on paper' matched her in real life.

Get a Head Start – Use a Template and Examples

If you are going to tackle writing or updating your own resume, use one of the hundreds of freely available templates on the internet. Do specific searches for your needs, e.g. 'career change resume template' and spend time reviewing those you find from the perspective of the person most likely to read your resume. This will give you ideas on current trends and do's/don'ts for writing your resume.

When you go to write your content, craft your professional summary, or create dot points on your recent experience, search the hundreds of examples on the internet. Do a specific search for content such as 'professional summary for customer service attendant' and review and adapt them again from the perspective of the person most likely to read this resume. There are a couple of examples of resumes at www.whatnowcareer.com/resources

References

Line your references up *before* job searching. Most organizations doing recruitment won't check references before deciding you've made the short list for interviews, and most will wait until you are a front-runner after interviews. However, occasionally your references may be requested up front, so you need to be ready by:

✓ **Decide on at least two referees**	Your two most recent supervisor/manager(s) are usually best, but sometimes this isn't possible. Don't panic! Consider other people that might be appropriate, for example, a work colleague, another manager from a different section of the organization, a person you have done volunteer work with, if you are a member of a committee in your free time (for example, a sporting club) then the chairperson of the committee.
✓ **Line up a variety of referees**	You may even line up a number of different referees, depending on the position or the industry you apply for. Offering a potential employer a variety of referees to choose from is a powerful statement.
✓ **Prime your referees**	Always make sure you check with your referees that they are (still) willing to provide a reference and then let them know of specific jobs that are likely to check your reference, so they are ready for the call. If possible, give them information about the organization and position (you might ask if they want to see the job description or advertisement).
✓ **Thank your referees**	Thank your referees profusely and often. Reference checks can be time consuming and onerous, some request written references, where the referee has to answer questions similar to selection criteria.

Use Informal Resumes

In the same way that you will want to research the organization and or the recruiter before applying for a job, it is common for people doing recruitment to research you.

- **LinkedIn** – Once your resume is done, get onto LinkedIn and make sure you have an attractive profile. If you are going to have a photo, make sure it's a professional one. And you can give a bit more information in your profile than in your resume. In fact, stepping a moment into the shoes of the person culling applications, they will most likely look up a candidate they're interested in, perhaps when they're trying to decide between you and another candidate to bring in for an interview. Don't just regurgitate your resume, give them a bit more to go on and something to set you apart.

- **Social media and internet presence** – Be aware of your social media presence and check what comes up if you do an internet search of your name. Be mindful that a keen recruiter may have a poke around to see what they can find about you.

Okay…. Done with resumes? Let's move onto Step 5 and the Job Application process. Once again, it's not about you, it's about them.

STEP 5

Writing Applications –
It's not about you, it's about them

Well here it comes, why I didn't land a job after 55 applications.

We've now arrived at one of the main reasons I didn't land a job through my 55 job applications, due in part to a complete absence of empathy for those doing the recruiting. And how I went from this utter failure to successfully employing my empathy and landing the first job I applied for after my return from maternity leave.

This may sound easy, just use empathy, but when I came across the advertisement for the job I landed, a whole lot of emotions arose – excitement, anxiety and a bit of panic. This seemed to be the perfect job as a first step to my new career, and it was flexible, local and part-time, so I could keep up with my parenting duties. I had no doubt this would be a highly competitive recruitment and my confidence in getting job interviews, or landing a job was very low.

I acknowledged my own feelings and then really stepped into the employer's shoes and thought about what they might want from the person in this job as a baseline, and what might really attract them, as a bonus.

Only when I felt I had a clear view did I start to put together an application.

> *Only when I felt I had a clear view did I start to put together an application.*

The ad called for only a resume to be sent through, but I composed a cover letter that clearly set out how I could do the job they wanted even though I'd never done it before, *and* what I could provide over and above, and outlined how I thought that could be of benefit in the role.

The employer called me shortly after I sent the application and we spoke for some time on the phone because he had been 'intrigued' by my application. He invited me in for an interview and offered me the job while I was there!

Your Written Application

Just as I did, before you put pen to paper, or more accurately fingers to keyboard, you need to step into the shoes of the person who will be culling the applications (the culler) – usually this is the same person who has received your resume.

The notions we've already explored regarding the reader of your resume, also hold for your written application. Namely, the culler may not be experienced, may have limited time and this may be outside of their core job. Not to mention being the recipient of many applications they need to cull down to just a handful to interview. How will they cull? How will they concentrate on that many written applications?

Written applications take a few different forms:
- ▶ a cover letter

- ▶ online application form, or
- ▶ a set of online questions

Whatever the format, essentially you need to tell the person culling the applications, in writing, why you think you are suited for their job.

The Aim of your Written Application

Let's first reposition your view of the written application by examining the aim for the culler. It's usually to decide out of all the applications who they will select for an interview, *not* who they are going to offer the job to. It is important to reiterate here that the person doing the culling may not be the person who will be interviewing. For example, in some organizations, the Human Resources Manager will cull the applications and send a short list of potential interview candidates to the position's direct manager, who then conducts interviews.

So, reordering this in your brain to change the value of the written application for you, its aim is to score you an interview. That's all. Not the much higher value of getting you the job, just to proceed to the next step in the recruitment process and be offered an interview.

Getting an Interview using a Written Application

Now the question simply becomes how to write an application that gives you a better chance to score an interview? And the answer is… there are lots of ways.

STEP 5 - Writing Applications – It's not about you, it's about them

Not only can you influence the culler to give you an interview, you have complete control over your written application. This can have a significant positive influence on your emotions.

> Not only can you influence the culler to give you an interview, you have complete control over your written application. This can have a significant positive influence on your emotions.

1. **Gather Information from the Advertisement**
   Read the job ad carefully and take note of key phrases or words in the ad. For example, "The position involves delivering outcomes in a *complex* and *sensitive environment*." Then repeat these in your written application. You might address your communication skills in your written application and describe your experience as, "In my previous role with the law courts, I was required to write Court Reports, formal documents delivered to the Magistrate and used during sentencing. The court system was *complex* to navigate in terms of how to structure the reports, and I would hand deliver these reports due to the *sensitive environment* where we dealt with information on offenders and victims of crime."

In this example, you have 'joined the dots' for the culler, and made their job easier. They don't have to try to think how your experience in the legal system relates to this position, as you've spelled it out for them using their own words.

Compare this to how inexperienced job application writers might approach this: "I have experience delivering outcomes in a complex and sensitive environment during my role with the law courts."

While this does repeat the words from the job ad, it's not effective as it tells the reader nothing — regardless of whether it is true or not. To make any sense of this, the culler would have to reference the resume to see what that job entailed, and then imagine how that might be relevant to this position. This is too much work for them to have to do, and mostly they won't do it.

> *So, your job is to describe (briefly) how what you have done before is similar to the requirements of this job, using their words wherever possible so they can recognize it easily.*

So, your job is to describe (briefly) how what you have done before is similar to the requirements of this job, using their words wherever possible so they can recognize it easily.

2. **Gather Information about the Organization**
   If you are not already familiar with the organization, you need to do a quick internet search on them We'll return to this later in more detail, but for now get a feel for the organization size, location, management structure, anything specific to the job. For example, if the position is in sales and marketing, you might research their current and historical sales position. You may be able to work some of this information into your written application.

3. **Gather Information about the Organization Contact**
   If there is a contact name in the job ad, you should also do a quick internet search (including LinkedIn) on this person. No, this is not creepy! You're not looking for anything in particular, just seeing if they have a profile on the internet if you don't know them, and you might get information on the person's own work history which may come in handy.

STEP 5 - Writing Applications – It's not about you, it's about them

For example, you might find the contact name is the direct manager and has only been in the position for a month. Now, while this doesn't tell you anything concrete, you may be able to use this information later on during an interview to build rapport.

4. **Call the Contact Person**
   This is the MOST important step! Once you've done your investigation, you need to call the contact person as soon as practicable. You'll do this even if you don't have any specific questions you want answered. While the information gathered from this contact may reap some useful information for your written application (remember we're trying to find anything that can be used to better tailor your resume and give your written application an edge), it can be *much* more powerful!

In this phone call, you start to build rapport with the contact person, and a personal relationship with the people involved in the recruitment. The power of this personal relationship should never be underestimated, it can even help you to land the job. Occasionally, there may only be an email address, and no phone number. Although it's more difficult to build rapport over email, it's still worth drafting a quick email to show extra effort.

	Calling the Contact Person Checklist	
1	This goes for any contact person listed on the job ad – don't make the mistake of not bothering if the contact person is someone you judge does not have influence over the job decision, for example, the manager's personal assistant, or the HR administrator. If you're effective with building rapport, you never know what that person might say to the actual recruiter when passing over your application to them. At the very least, the culler will register your name as familiar in the pile of resumes for unknown applicants and this will cause them to look a little closer at your application.	✓
2	The reason for your call will be to ask questions about the role, so any genuine questions you have regarding the organization or the job are best. If you can't think of anything you want to ask, or you only have one question and want a couple more to keep the person on the phone to better build rapport, I've listed a few below. • *What do you think are the major challenges for the role?* • *What's the manager's/person in charge's/head of department's, etc most important priority for the team, and for the role?* • *What is the structure of the team I will be managing/working in, how does it fit within the department/organization?* • *Can you describe the culture of the organization/culture of the team and department (or how would other people describe it)?* • *Can you give me an idea of the breakdown of the role, (e.g. how much is managing, how much is technical)?* If you do decide to use some of these, remember to practice them first. Say them out loud *before* getting on the phone – does the phrasing of the question sound like you? Would you use these words, or would you say something slightly different? If it sounds strange or doesn't sit well with you, then reword it to suit.	✓

STEP 5 - Writing Applications – It's not about you, it's about them

3	When you're on the phone, have paper and pen handy so you can jot some of the words and phrases they use or their answers, so you don't forget them because you're nervous having to call the person and trying to make a good impression! You can use them later in your written application (along with phrases from the job ad).	✓
4	Don't be too 'professional' or rigid during the phone call. You want to stand out so they look more closely at your application when it arrives. Try to let a little of you shine through if you think that's appropriate, but take your cues from the person on the other end of the phone. For example, if they sound rushed and a bit curt, chances are the last thing they need is your phone call at this moment! Ask if this is a good time to have a chat about the position and offer to call back at a better time if it's not.	✓

Pulling it all together

Now you've gathered all your information, you're ready to put together the application itself, so let's get to it. This might be another time you ask someone to help out. Having someone experienced in writing effective cover letters and selection criteria responses write your first application can give you a template to base your future ones on and make your job easier. Here are some essentials:

1. **Meet specific instructions** – You need to make absolutely sure you meet any specific instructions. An example might be to provide a cover letter, so do that. It might be to address a number of selection criteria, so make sure you do it. It might be to provide a cover letter addressing the selection criteria in no more than two pages, so make sure you don't exceed the two-page mark. In my experience, it's not uncommon for the culler to immediately discard those applications not meeting something they have asked for, without looking at the resume or any other part of the application. They make a judgement

about you immediately – you're lazy, no attention to detail, don't care enough about the job to put effort in – whatever that judgement, and no matter how wrong, it ultimately makes their job of culling easier. Some recruiters employ software to do some of these tasks for them. For example, they ask the software to ignore all applications that have a higher word count than they have requested. An extra 2 words above their requested word count in any one of your answers to selection criteria, could cost you that job because your application is not even considered.

> *An extra 2 words above their requested word count in any one of your answers to selection criteria, could cost you that job because your application is not even considered.*

2. **Cover Letter** – Do a cover letter EVERY time, even if not explicitly requested. There are many reasons why you should do this. The only reason why you wouldn't would be that you might waste your time because they might not read it if they haven't expressly asked for one – that would be rare. Providing a cover letter when it's not requested will show enthusiasm, as you have put extra effort in, and they will most likely read it if you've provided it.

3. **Selection Criteria** – Always respond to selection criteria in some way, regardless of whether they are explicit in the ad, or they are 'hidden' in the Position or Job Description, or you have to guess what they might be. For example, often the Job Description will have a section listing 'Job Duties' or 'Essential Skills' or something listing criteria similar to those you would find listed in a job ad. Even if selection criteria are listed in the ad, these sections can give you additional information to utilize in your responses, in the same way

as described previously you can utilize actual words or phrases found in the Job Description in your application. In a worst-case scenario, if absolutely none are available, put forward the three things you think would be the most important for the job and how you fit these. This is where your earlier research – looking at the organization on the internet, calling the contact person and asking them about the job, etc – comes into play. You'll have additional information to stand in their shoes and give your best educated guess as to what they are looking for in this job.

The Cover Letter

Let's spend a minute considering the cover letter while standing in the shoes of the recruiter, to help you reposition this task. Let's say they get a package including a cover letter, selection criteria responses and a resume. The most logical way of viewing this package is to read the cover letter first.

The aim of the cover letter is to capture attention, so they are drawn to open your selection criteria or resume. In detail:

1. The cover letter is not just a 'container' to gather everything together and put some contact details in – which is how it's often treated. You are trying to make a personal connection with the person culling the applications. So, it's appropriate to write about your enthusiasm and passion for the job/organization, and your personal values and how they match the organization; those things that showcase you and what you offer, but you won't necessarily cover in detail in other parts of your written application.

2. Because you're trying to raise the culler's curiosity to open your resume and selection criteria, you want to stand out a little in the cover letter and cover the MOST important points about your experience or skills as they pertain to this job. Make the recruiter's job as easy as possible, and make them hopeful that when they open your other documents you are going to be the perfect interview candidate.

3. Use whatever information you have to tailor your cover letter to the organization, and the culler. If you provide this additional information in an explicit way, this will make it easier for the culler to identify and recognize the additional effort you have gone to for this position. For example, you might write in the cover letter, "As discussed with Sandra Brown, one of the main challenges with this position has been identified as managing the numerous stakeholders with different agendas. My experience in XYZ role directly relates to this, where I ....". In this sentence, you've reminded them that you called the contact person and have also responded to the information collected, even if it wasn't listed as a criterion for selection.

4. Think carefully about information you've found out through your investigations and what you might include of that in your cover letter. For example, a focus on the values of the organization in the advertisement, shows this may be very important to them, even if it's not listed specifically in the selection criteria. You would be well served to at least mention this or focus on values as a theme through your cover letter.

5. Generally, cullers are drawn to select people genuinely excited about this opportunity – the job and the organization. Now, I have an expectation you're not going to know some of the organizations you are applying for jobs at, and there is also a high probability that not all organizations are going to knock your socks off with excitement at the prospect of working there. But you need to find some element of excitement, so you can

communicate it genuinely in your cover letter. You need to use your investigations to find an authentic enthusiasm and passion for the organization and/or job you're applying for. Sometimes this is the hardest bit of a job application. Once you have found that, you need to find a way to communicate this excitement. Simply writing, "I am excited to present my application for XYZ role within ABC organization" even if you are, does not communicate genuine enthusiasm and excitement. Instead try something like, "I am truly excited by this role, and I'm delighted I may be able to bring my diverse experience, skills and knowledge to an area that is a personal passion of mine, bringing accounting knowledge to assist an organization to realize efficiencies in their operations."

> When you write your cover letter, you can search hundreds of examples on the internet and review and adapt them from the perspective of the culler. I have provided a number of examples at www.whatnowcareer.com/resources

Responding to Selection Criteria

You are always going to address selection criteria in some form, it might be in a separate statement, an online form with questions for you to answer, or if none are provided you are going to 'find' them or assume a few and answer them.

1. As with everything you are doing in this process, you are trying to make the job of the culler as easy as possible. So, if you are asked to respond specifically to selection criteria,
    - list them as headings and
    - write your answers underneath each heading. That way they will be able to easily identify that you have addressed all requirements, rather than hunting through a freeform discussion of your skills and experience.

2. As already mentioned, make sure you use their terminology wherever possible. So, if they talk time management skills, this is what you will refer to, even though you might think of them as organizational skills.

When you start writing selection criteria responses, you can search hundreds of examples on the internet and review and adapt them from the perspective of the culler. I have provided a number of examples at www.whatnowcareer.com/resources

Addressing Potential Obstacles

In your written application you need to explicitly address any obstacles you imagine may be in your way to landing this job or may make you a less attractive candidate for an interview.

Kathy's Story

Let's take Kathy who took a career break to look after her aging parent and had been out of the workforce for a few years. Her resume, when she first came to me, had no work history for the past three years. If a culler received this resume, they would most likely notice the gap. And if she did not address this gap explicitly, it would be natural for the culler to make some judgements, and that could be anything, from wondering if she took time off to start a family, or she had burnout and had three years stress leave, or she was on welfare for three years because she was unemployable.

Whatever their imaginings, this posed a very real obstacle for Kathy. If it came down to her and another application where there were no question marks over their work experience, the culler would likely choose the other to interview.

STEP 5 - Writing Applications – It's not about you, it's about them

It's preferable to be upfront with the recruiter and address the obstacle and why it should not be counted as such. If they don't like your truthful reasoning, or accept it but still see it as an obstacle, it's better to be culled out at that stage.

There are a number of ways to address obstacles.

1. You might choose to put this experience on your resume, particularly if it might be an asset for your next move. In Kathy's case she decided to move from her previous career and look to get into aged care. The experience of caring for her parent, although not a paid, formal job was a real benefit to entering this new career, and she highlighted this on her resume.

2. You can address the obstacle(s) in the cover letter. If you choose to do this, it will be toward the end of the letter, *after* you have had a chance to 'sell' yourself and generate their interest about you. In Kathy's case, she addressed the obstacle of no formal qualification in aged care at the end of her cover letter, by highlighting her practical experience, her passion for providing this care through her experience and her willingness to undertake study if required.

Saving your Sanity, and a Little Time

There is no getting away from the fact that writing cover letters and selection criteria is time consuming, even if you are experienced and skilled at it. It's sometimes daunting when over 10 criteria are listed and you need to answer them all in under two pages. And it's sometimes frustrating, as when three completely unrelated criteria are rolled into one, for example, "Criteria 2: Time management, organizational and negotiation skills". As you do more written applications it can also be a source of frustration when they are worded slightly differently to one you have already written, for example, "High level communication skills" versus "Oral and written communication skills". Here they definitely overlap but take time to tweak.

To help manage this frustration and lessen the workload, create a simple database using a word processor or spreadsheet application, or whatever you're comfortable with. This way you can easily search for different responses you have already put together and use them as a starting point. It might look like this:

Category	Topic {Actual criteria}	Response {copy & paste applications}
Communication	Oral and written communication skills	…
	High level communication skills	…
	Exceptional Interpersonal skills	…
Cover Letter	Obstacle – career break 3 years	…
Qualifications	Bachelor of Business (or equivalent experience)	…

You can download a free template for the Job Application Response Database here www.whatnowcareer.com/resources

STEP 5 - Writing Applications – It's not about you, it's about them

If you're going to go to all the effort of writing them, you might as well reuse them. You can also use the database to store anything else that is reusable, for example, a generic closing paragraph for your cover letter. Start at your very first job application – believe me, you'll thank me! When you write the first couple of applications you might think it's easier and less time-consuming to retrieve a bit from last week's application. As you write more, or you are on the job hunt again in the future, it is MUCH easier to look in the one place for these and do a quick search for what you're after.

As you write each application, copy and paste the different responses into their respective place in your Selection Criteria database ready for the next application. And add every single criteria you do, even if you can't imagine ever needing to reuse it. It doesn't take a lot of time and you never know when you might need it, and the frustration of remembering you've written something like that somewhere before is excruciating!

And now to the culmination of all your efforts so far. Whether or not you love the interview process or hate it, you are going to get there eventually!

KIRSTEN BRUMBY

STEP 6

*Landing that job or career with
a great interview –
Be your best you*

Hands down my most uncomfortable interview experience happened when I went for my first government contract.

Totally unprepared as to what to expect, I walked into a roundtable of six chairs, with four men and a woman already seated. The coordinator asked me to sit and then introduced each person by name and title. Then he said there were five questions and each person would read one in turn. He read the first question, and that was it. There was absolutely no attempt at building rapport, at all.

I had no non-verbal cues whatsoever from any of the five, no verbal acknowledgements either, and there were no follow-up questions. I would simply finish talking, and then the next person would read their question. I had no eye contact as all five madly wrote down everything I said.

With no acknowledgement of any kind, I felt less confident with every answer I gave. I imagined my answers were not hitting the mark for any of them.

STEP 6 - Landing that job or career with a great interview – Be your best you

> *I left the interview room feeling awful and not sure how I had managed to screw up the interview so badly. I was upset with myself because I really wanted that contract.*

I left the interview room feeling awful and not sure how I had managed to screw up the interview so badly. I was upset with myself because I really wanted that contract.

To my complete and utter surprise and delight, I received an email shortly after saying I had landed the job! However, I couldn't reconcile my terrible performance in the interview with then getting the job. Fast forward a couple of years and, through my work in the contract, I had built relationships with some of the interviewers in attendance that day. I shared with them how awful it was for me, and they explained that at the time they had just implemented a new process for recruitment, where panel interviews had to be conducted, and all interviews had to be carried out exactly the same to ensure fairness (no additional questions were allowed).

A strict regime of having no bias toward any applicant was implemented, and they had to record all their observations in a complicated template and then score each question's response, to provide evidence for their selection.

They had all just received training in order to be able to do the interviews, some had never interviewed anyone before, and all of them were terrified of making a mistake. I was one of the first interviews, and they still had about 20 people to interview. Whoa! I was blown away. I'd had no idea.

I hadn't spared a thought for the interviewers, let alone spent some time in their shoes. I felt the people conducting the interview had all the power because they were awarding the job. I saw them as sitting in a place of confidence, when that was not anywhere close to the truth. I needed to reset my expectations of interviewers. As soon as I heard what they had been through, I felt nothing but sympathy for them.

> *I needed to reset my expectations of interviewers.*

There are many other possible scenarios; the interviewer may feel ill-prepared, nervous, and under the pump trying to squeeze this additional task into their already busy workload. They may feel worried about the responsibility of finding the 'right' person and already starting to feel bad about rejecting seven of the eight people they interview.

I was somehow lucky to perform adequately for that particular job, however, my distress could have been significantly lessened and my performance could have been enhanced had I considered for even a moment what might have been going on for my interviewers.

I never thought that there might be another reason for their behavior, besides me giving bad answers to their questions. Going into an interview feeling a genuine curiosity for the interviewer's situation and a little compassion for them, and the job they have to do, can help reposition the interview for you, giving a whole new perspective on them and their behavior during the interview. This can also help you reinterpret the interview as a less threatening event.

There is another view you might hold about the interviewer without realizing. You may see the interviewer as an adversary, or as David Rock, in his book *Your Brain at Work*, refers to as a 'foe'.

STEP 6 - Landing that job or career with a great interview – Be your best you

David contends your brain functions change when perceiving someone as a foe, you will feel less (or no) empathy for them and therefore produce less oxytocin (a hormone which can help you feel calm and ease stress). This means you will have a less pleasant interaction.

The good news is that an initial bit of rapport building in an interview can help you to feel more connected and make all the difference because oxytocin will be released. So, get good at the first part of interviews, and you'll have a better chance of enjoying the rest of the interview and performing well.

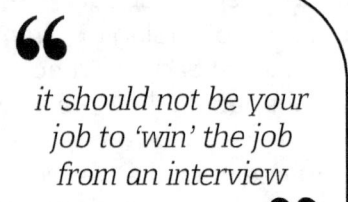

> *it should not be your job to 'win' the job from an interview*

Having said that, it should not be your job to 'win' the job from an interview, and this belief can apply additional pressure. Let's swing this around the right way – it's the interviewer's 'job' to select the best person for the job at the end of interviewing all candidates. This means it's their job and their responsibility to get the most out of you in the interview. But, just as many people attending interviews are not good at showcasing themselves, there are many interviewers who are not good at making sure they see the 'real' person in an interview (the person they would be in the job, without the stress caused by the interview).

In fact, many interviewers are inexperienced or just don't have sufficient interviewing skills. The interviewer may only need to hire a handful of people in their working life, so might not have the chance to develop the skill.

The (Real) Aim of the Interview, for the Interviewer

What is the interviewer actually trying to achieve in the interview? What is their aim?

For many interviewers, the hidden (subconscious) aim is to make a judgement of whether the candidate will fit in the team/organization, and if they'll like working with them. To a lesser degree (usually), they will be trying to figure out if you will be able to do the job, and to what extent.

That's taken care of by your resume and written application which got you here in the first place, and some recruitment processes will include a separate 'technical' interview, psychometric testing, competency-based questions asked verbally, or in writing, to prove your capability.

With this in mind then, if you put on a facade during the interview, being someone you are not, then you are in effect falsely advertising yourself. If you get the job based on this other 'persona' you may potentially struggle with Imposter Syndrome. Imposter Syndrome, when starting a new job, refers to the feeling that you're a fake and don't deserve to have been offered the job, and can even cause you to feel you're not up to the task at hand. Also, in the actual interview, unless you happen to be a seasoned actor, putting on this façade will take a whole lot of brain energy better dedicated to intelligently answering questions.

You need to let them see who you really are, not some persona you put on for interviews. Be authentic but be the best 'you' that you can be.

STEP 6 - Landing that job or career with a great interview – Be your best you

Lucy's story

What do I mean by letting them see the real you? Let me give you the example of Lucy, who was a compulsive note taker during meetings, made lists, and diligently prepared for everything. One of the things making her nervous about interviews was when the interviewer asked if she had any questions, she would draw a blank. All of the things she had been curious about before the interview — the job, the organization and the team — were gone. She would get flustered and answer, "No, I think you've answered all my questions." Leaving the interview, she would be disappointed, knowing she should have asked at least one question to show her interest in the job.

Even when they had answered all her questions, Lucy would feel she was sending the message she didn't care enough about the job to ask questions, or she hadn't communicated her enthusiasm for working with the organization, as it looked like she hadn't prepared for the interview.

My suggestion for Lucy was to work on a technique that would not only make her feel better in the interview (and as a result, perform better), but would highlight one of her strengths to a prospective employer. I encouraged Lucy to write in her notebook her preparatory research on the organization, as well as the questions she had for them. She then brought the notebook into interviews. I also had her work on a script helping her to be comfortable doing something not normally done in interviews. When asked whether she had any questions, Lucy would now confidently reply, "You might have answered them all, but

I'll just check the ones I wrote down before the interview" and would then pull out the notebook, clearly tagged to the right page and read the questions she had prepared earlier.

She practiced this before her next interview and used it from then on until she successfully landed her job. She reported that it didn't just affect that part of the interview, but she was able to relax throughout the full interview, even enjoy talking about herself, as she didn't have to worry she was going to forget her questions.

Now, think what Lucy has done. Firstly, she's done what is not normal in an interview. So, what! Who made that a rule? That you can't pull out a notebook and reference something? By NOT remembering, she showcased a potential 'weakness' - poor memory (even if not strictly true). And unless the job you're going for requires an exceptional memory, referencing a notebook will do more positive things than just supporting you to be the best you.

The interviewer will not only likely recognize your prior preparation, but also get a better feeling for who you will be at work, that is, the one who prepares before meetings and takes notes, and doesn't forget things because you write them down. If you felt this would be a benefit to the job you're going for – I'd bring out the notebook even if you're sure they have answered all your questions, just so they see it.

Using Lucy as an excellent example, what can you do when faced with a prospective interview? Think about what you do, or don't do, during an interview, what you say and don't say, and what that might or might not communicate to the interviewer.

STEP 6 - Landing that job or career with a great interview – Be your best you

Think about what you really want to communicate in the interview that you believe is important to the interviewer and to the job. And what are ways you can show this, rather than just answering a question about it.

Another example might be if they mention a sense of humor in the advertisement, to let this shine in the interview (don't be too much of a try-hard though). Don't forget, they are judging whether they like you and will enjoy working with you – they are either going to like your sense of humor, or they're not.

Before you do anything

Before worrying about what your objective is for the interview, I'd like you to take a quiet moment to acknowledge and recognize your achievement. The aim of you writing an application for a job was an interview, and you have done that! Well done! Allow yourself to feel the flush of success, maybe open your written application and have a read through your cover letter and selection criteria. You have done a good job with it, enjoy this moment.

The Aim of the Interview, for You

I often ask my coaching clients what they think the aim of a job interview is, and I mostly get a funny look as an answer and in the ensuing silence will add 'to get a job, of course'. But in my book, literally and figuratively, this is not an aim, it is actually no more than a pleasant and welcome potential outcome.

Given the interviewer mainly wants to figure out if they want to work with you, if you can leave an interview feeling they have seen the authentic you (and haven't made a complete mess of ALL the questions), then that's all you can ask of yourself – and that, therefore, is your aim.

If you achieve this new aim and DON'T secure the job, you can rest peacefully in the knowledge you have done your job well and there's nothing more you could have done. For some reason, you will most likely never know, they liked someone else better for the role or there was someone else with better experience suited to the job. Furthermore, and importantly for you, if the interviewer has had the opportunity to see the 'real you' and doesn't offer you the job because they don't like what they see, then chances are you wouldn't like working there anyway, so much better not to be selected at this stage.

There is a secondary aim for interviews, and that is for you to interview the interviewer. I have found a deep-seated belief, which is rarely challenged because it is seldom brought to the surface, that the interviewer holds all the power, and they are like some king or queen sitting on their throne knighting people with jobs. This belief is disempowering and offers nothing but a sense of hopelessness about your ability to really influence the decision.

We can change the belief that the interviewer holds the power by accepting a deceptively simple idea - an interview is a two-way street. Really!

No matter how desperate you are for this job, one of your aims for the interview is to find out if you *want* the job. You need to interview the organization just as closely as they are interviewing

STEP 6 - Landing that job or career with a great interview – Be your best you

you. If you can self-cull during an interview, and decide *you* don't want the job, it's preferable to taking the job because you haven't considered this at all and realizing within a short space of time it's not the place for you.

This new belief and aim provide you more to focus on during the interview, rather than how you fluffed the last question. It can relieve some of the pressure off how *you* are acting in the interview, shifting your focus onto how *they* are behaving. So now you have a dual aim for the interview – to make sure the 'real you' is present and to pay attention to, and interview, the interviewer.

Getting Better at Interviews – Improving your Skills

If you've reached this point and still find that you don't like interviews very much, you need to ask yourself Why is that? What is it EXACTLY about interviews you don't like? Think of some interviews you've done; what are the bits you feel didn't go well, or what is it sticking in your mind about why certain interviews were so awful? What's the part you're not good at? What's the bit you fear the most?

The F Word

Fear…aah, there…. I've gone and said the 'F' word. It's got to be said, because if you're honest with yourself, the bit(s) you don't like, or the general dislike you have for interviews, probably have their roots in some kind of fear. Even if it's just the low-lying fear of somehow messing up this golden opportunity, or a general fear of being rejected.

Susan Jeffers, in her book *Feel the Fear and do it anyway*, says, "The only way to get rid of the fear of doing something is to go out and do it."

The good news is you can practice dealing with the fear, before you go to an actual interview. You need to identify the parts that generate fear and then practice those scenarios. If you are not good at the introductions, practice with someone else by just walking into a room, shaking their hand and introducing yourself. If you fear your mind going blank when you're asked a difficult question, then get someone to ask you difficult questions and practice responding to them on the spot.

1. *I don't feel comfortable in interviews*
Preparing for the interview before you get there will help you improve your interview skills.

    a) If you have the Job Description, make sure you familiarize yourself with it. And use this knowledge if you can in the interview. So, when answering a question, for example, 'What are your strengths?', you can choose one that fits the job description and mention it is not only your strength, but from your knowledge of the position, you imagine it will come in handy.

    b) For particular jobs you can prepare generically for some of the implied role duties. For example, for general management positions you can prepare the main areas of management – finance, human resources, strategic planning, etc – making sure you can summarize what is involved in each and your experience in them. Then whatever question they throw at you in the interview, you will have a scaffold from which to confidently hang your answer.

    c) Make sure you prepare at least two to three questions to ask the interviewer. You will ALWAYS ask at least one question at the end of the interview, because this demonstrates preparation and enthusiasm.

2. *I don't seem to get the interview off to a good start*
Often, if you get through the introductions of an interview with confidence, a positive tone is set and you can relax and answer

questions more effectively. This is why it's so important for interviewers to build rapport and set you at ease at the start of an interview. As we've already discussed, this doesn't always happen! You can take control of this aspect in the opening minutes of the interview if the interviewer does not, and work to build rapport with the interviewer.

There are many simple rapport building techniques you can use to find a connection with them, such as smiling, holding eye contact and finding some common ground.

Labeling

One technique that will benefit you, and the interviewer, is expressing any emotions happening for you in the moment. In other words, if you feel nervous, tell the interviewer you feel nervous. Neuroscience has identified the concept of 'labeling' which is when you feel an emotion, to give it a label and articulate it.

a) Firstly, it has been shown that trying not to feel the emotion doesn't work. Have you ever tried to talk yourself out of being nervous before an interview?

b) Secondly, if you try to suppress the emotion, all the resources in your brain will be directed toward this, rather than answering interview questions. If, on the other hand, you label the emotion, it can help to dampen the arousal in your brain and make the emotion easier to manage.

c) Finally, and arguably the most important reason, is you can actually make the interviewer uncomfortable. It's been shown that when we observe something in someone else, that mirror neurons (specific nerve cells) in our own brain fire exactly as if we are experiencing it ourselves. It's why we yawn when we see someone else yawn. So, the interviewer's mirror neurons pick up you are nervous, and their brain may then react as if they are nervous! If you don't tell them, they may not register that it is your nervousness they have just picked up on, and just have a feeling of disquiet or unease about you.

3. I don't give a good first impression

There has been much research into, and more written about, the science of first impressions. There are differences in the findings about how many seconds it takes to form that first impression, with seven often quoted. However long that tiny timeframe, it definitely happens in the opening minute of the interview.

The good news for you is that you can control how you are when you first enter the interview room, or the interviewer comes and fetches you. Your introduction can be practiced and developed as a skill, and this, according to Tyler Tervooren in his article *The Art and Science of Making Great First Impressions (https://riskology.co/first-impression/)* , is what you're looking to develop:

a) Strong eye contact (but not staring)
b) A firm handshake that is warm and dry
c) An authoritative voice (firm, not too soft, not too loud)
d) Similar dress style (people want to know you're like them, not better than them)
e) Clean, healthy teeth (check you've nothing from lunch stuck there)
f) Tall, open posture (relaxed but no slumping – chin up, arms at your side, back straight)

Setting a good first impression can be more difficult if you are faced with a virtual interview. If you are required to participate in a video or phone interview, giving a good first impression is just as essential as it is in a face-to-face interview. The key to this is prior preparation. Test your technology, make sure you have a quiet space and check your lighting and background. Dress for success, as if you were meeting in person and when you are on the call all of the above still hold. Keep eye contact as much as possible, even looking at the camera from time to time rather than at the images of interviewers on the screen. Sit up straight and in an open posture.

So, get practicing!

4. I'm not comfortable talking about myself

So, you don't like talking about yourself or feel you're bragging or being boastful when talking about your strengths and achievements? Get over it! This is what an interview is about, and you need to do it well. Interestingly, the science says we spend 60% of conversations talking about ourselves, and research has indicated this is because talking about ourselves is pleasurable – it stimulates areas of the brain and feelings associated with things such as good food, sex and using drugs.[1]

Even if you don't believe the science relates to you, you can always develop it as a skill. And to develop it is pretty easy – practice, practice, and then some more practice.

So how do you practice?

By doing it! In an interview, you will commonly have the opportunity to respond to five key areas. Even though they may be asked in different forms during an interview, the responses you develop and practice can be used often. Your responses must be authentic and show the 'real you'. Genuine and honest answers here are possible and essential. And when they are delivered confidently (because you've practiced them), will come across authentically to the interviewer.

	5 key responses to prepare	
1	2-minute elevator pitch – this is a very brief description of what your unique 'selling points' are.	(An 'elevator pitch' refers to the idea of being in a lift with a person you want to influence and having only the length of the elevator ride to tell them everything in a nutshell.)
2	3-minute summary of your career.	
3	3-minute summary of who you are and what you are passionate about at work.	Your knowledge, skills, attributes, experience.
4	Your key strengths – 2 minutes.	
5	Your weaknesses – 2 minutes.	

You can prepare these before interviews and learn them, so they roll off your tongue smoothly when you use them in an interview. To get you started, lots of examples can be found by a basic internet search.

5. I'm no good at answering questions on the spot

If you find it difficult to answer questions 'on the spot' in an interview, it will help if you can practice answering lots of different questions by writing 'scripts' and then reading them out loud multiple times. You will never be able to guess every question that might be asked, so the real skill here is to develop your ability to answer questions on the spot. You've already started the process by developing and practicing the scripts to talk about yourself, and you can then utilize these answers for multiple questions.

Identifying other common questions or things you are likely to cover, or areas you are weak in, and practicing generic answers to these will help. For example, say you work in management, and finance is not a strong point for you. If you've prepared some answers on working with budgets and reporting, in the interview you will have a start point for any finance related question. Then if you do get a question in one of your weaker spots, you are less likely to panic and draw a blank, and as a bonus, you will appear confident.

You might also practice responses around the job requirements, for example if the job advertisement emphasizes that the role deals with conflict, and negotiation skills are an essential criteria, then you could prepare an example from your work life where you've dealt with conflict and used negotiation skills, how you did this and what the result was.

And here's the formula!

While practicing, consider the following formula for answering questions that can be applied to almost every question you are asked. Through practice, you can get used to answering every question using the formula and this can provide you an automatic scaffold in an interview to answer a difficult or unexpected question.

YOUR ANSWER = Generic statement + example + positive outcomes

Using this formula, you will always give an example, always make a general statement about how you normally do things or experience/knowledge you have that helps, and you will always link these to positive outcomes/results.

For example, if you are asked:

> "Give me an example of a time you led a high performing team and what you achieved.".

This is clearly asking for an example, so you explain your example, including the positive result from the situation,

> "I lead a high performing team at the moment, we are responsible for xxx and when I took this team on I met with each person individually, blah blah blah… and now we are exceeding our targets, and have been able to seamlessly integrate the work required for the additional caseload."

AND THEN you add to the end

> "This is how I lead teams in general, my leadership style is collaborative, I like to involve the team in decision making to help them take ownership and find our outcomes are effectively met and exceeded."

If they were to ask a different question you could use the same answer, for example,

> "How would you describe your management style?"

In this example, you would answer the generic answer first, THEN FOLLOW with an example, and end with the positive result:

> "In general terms, my leadership style is collaborative, I like to involve the team in decision making to help them take ownership and find our outcomes are effectively met and exceeded. For example, I lead a high performing team at the moment, we are responsible for xxx and when I took this team on I met with each person individually, blah blah blah… and now we are exceeding our targets, and have

been able to seamlessly integrate the work required for the additional caseload."

> If you need some ideas for questions to consider in preparation, a quick internet search will find you thousands. I have provided a few practice favorites at www.whatnowcareer.com/resources

6. I am scared of getting stuck on a question in the interview

It is really common to feel stuck at some point in an interview. It could be you freeze and cannot think, or you get lost in an answer and then don't know if you actually answered the question, or the answer to a question doesn't come easily to you. Here are some suggestions to combat stuckness:

1. Don't freak out! It's totally normal, so expect it to happen. Part of the horror of feeling stuck in an interview is the panic when you feel it happening that shuts down your brain and makes it difficult to recover from.

2. Try taking a deep breath and deliberately don't focus on the question for a few seconds. Just focus on taking that breath and releasing it. And be uncomfortably comfortable in the silence. A bit of silence following a question is absolutely fine.

3. If you get stuck with a question somewhere – don't be afraid to tell that to the interviewer.

    a. Remember the labeling technique. Give whatever feeling that's happening for you in that moment a label, and then tell the interviewer. Examples are, "I feel a bit lost with that" or "I feel a bit confused by that question".

    b. If you get lost you can ask, "Have I answered the

question?" or "Does that answer the question?" You can use this as an opportunity to let your best you shine, for example, "Sorry, I seem to have rambled on a bit, but I get a bit passionate about this! Did that answer your question, or did I miss the point?" OR a bit of self-deprecating humor, "Okay, I'm just going to stop rambling now. Sorry about that."

c. You can ask, "Is that enough or would you like me to expand?" or "I'm not sure I've captured that succinctly, was that clear?"

The bottom line is, you will survive interviews, and messing up one question may not lose you the job, in fact depending on how you handle the mess up you've made, it can be an opportunity to be your best you!

In the next step, I move onto the secret ingredient, persistence, is the key to your success. Always looking at each application or interview as an opportunity to learn.

STEP 7

The Secret Ingredients – Persistence, perseverance and preparation

Unlike me, blithely expecting to be snapped up as soon as I submitted my first job application and being sorely disappointed by this misguided expectation, you've set your expectations to go through the whole process a few times before landing a job.

In order to keep doing everything you need to do, you are going to need to hone your skills and exercise persistence and tenacity.

Shama's story

Shama did just this. During coaching, she applied for a job within her skillset, but without the exact experience required in the sector. She followed the process I've outlined in previous steps, and on seeing the job advertisement, called the person doing the recruitment (the direct manager).

She struck up an instant rapport with the manager and shared her hesitation to apply for the role given she did not have direct experience in the sector. The manager encouraged her to apply for the role regardless, which

STEP 7 - The Secret Ingredients – Persistence, perseverance and preparation

she did and was confident of getting an interview. When she was informed by email she was not selected for an interview, Shama felt disappointed and angry she had wasted her time putting together a difficult application trying to adequately demonstrate her transferable skills.

In the end, she had only done so because of the manager's encouragement. After waiting a week (and for her anger to subside), she decided to follow up with the manager and ask for feedback. Upon calling, the manager's immediate response was, "I'm so glad you called!" and went on to explain they'd received more applications than they had expected, many with direct experience, and that was why she had not gained an interview. The manager then went on to explain they had identified a new position and they would very much like Shama to apply for it as they thought it would fit her perfectly. Shama did apply and won this role.

Don't be like me all those years ago, refusing to seek feedback and sinking into a depression. Instead, be like Shama. Acknowledge and accept emotions such as anger and disappointment that arise during the process and stay resilient.

Ask for feedback to improve your applications and follow the process.

Feedback and Continual Improvement

To improve the skills you need to land a job, you need to get feedback on them – and yes, I hear you groaning!

These are skills you are developing, and you need to improve them, at least until you land your new job. And you can only improve if you are able to judge what you did well and what you might do differently next time.

You're pretty normal if you feel asking for feedback following a failed job application or an unsuccessful interview is VERY hard. BUT it has the potential for so much more than just the feedback, and that makes it worth the discomfort and additional time. In addition to Shama landing her job as a direct result of her asking for feedback, there are further surprising results possible:

1. You may get constructive and useful feedback about your application wording, or how you were in the interview, which you can then assimilate and incorporate into your next attempts. Unfortunately, this is probably the least likely benefit. The primary reasons for this are people generally don't like giving feedback, are not good at it, and are uncomfortable giving perceived 'negative' feedback especially to someone they have rejected. Sometimes there is no specific reason as to why you were culled, or why someone else was hired. I think this is a sign of a poor recruiting process, but it is what it is, and your job-search-life is going to be easier if you can accept that it just is.

2. If you have put a lot of work into a written application, feel you've done a good job of it and don't get an interview, even if the chance of getting constructive feedback may be remote, asking can at least give you some satisfaction in holding the recruiter accountable for their decision not to get you in for an interview. Now I realize this may sound a little unsympathetic to the recruiter, but it can help your ability to feel in control, accept the rejection and let that application go to move on to the next.

3. You can continue to build a relationship with the person that has done the recruitment. You won't know if you were runner

up and what might happen at the end of the probation period and whether the person hired will work out. They may well get in contact to see if you're still available. You never know where this might lead, even to landing a new job.

When asking for feedback, it can be easier (for you and the person) to seek specific feedback, rather than requesting 'some feedback'. Ask specific questions about your performance in the interview, or your written application, and if you get stuck, consider these:

- Were there any questions where my answers could have been better/clearer?
- What could I have done differently?
- What did I do well?
- What could I do differently next time?

Self-evaluation

Written application – Once you've received some feedback, have a look through your written application and see if you can evaluate your own attempt. What might you do differently next time? What did you do well?

Interview – Following an interview, don't wait to be told the outcome of the interview, try to evaluate how *you* think you went. What do you need to practice more, what worked well for you, did you feel fear during the interview, if so when, and how did you deal with it?

Troubleshooting

Keep an eye out for patterns emerging in your feedback and do some troubleshooting. For example, you may get a high rate of interviews, but haven't landed a job yet; or you have done quite a few written applications and not landed an interview. If nothing changes, nothing changes. That is, if you are not getting interviews and don't change how you're writing your applications, you are unlikely to change the pattern of not getting an interview either.

If nothing changes, nothing changes.

Take the Long View

By now you should be comfortable with the notion that writing an application or doing an interview is not just about landing THIS job. Taking a long view of this process is useful and energizing, rather than being draining and depressing. The whole process can be about so much more than just landing this job and while that is your ultimate aim, other potential outcomes are:

1. Transferable skill and attitude development in the areas of:
    a. Writing skills
    b. Ability to 'sell' yourself, talk about your strengths and your experience and skills
    c. Confidence
    d. Resilience
    e. Tenacity
2. The potential to land another job, if not this one. Don't underestimate the power of any job application or your performance in an interview to influence your future. Expect unexpected future opportunities to arise out of a failed application, I have seen it so often that I do!
3. Build your networks for job opportunities, now and in the future. Recruitment agents are a great example of the importance of this.

STEP 7 - The Secret Ingredients – Persistence, perseverance and preparation

---

Mark's story

With a long work history of changing jobs and a generally poor view of recruitment agents, Mark called a specialist recruitment agent to discuss a position advertised on a job search website. After taking the effort to build rapport with the agent and discussing the position, Mark decided not to apply for that job and advised the agent. The agent still invited Mark in to meet them in the office to get to know him better. Although he thought it a waste of time, Mark agreed. The meeting took place and Mark further developed the relationship with the agent, discussing his job requirements and wishes (from his *Drop-Dead List*).

Within two weeks of the meeting, the agent called Mark to discuss a three-month contract at an organization that fitted his requirements. The job was not advertised anywhere yet and following a brief conversation, Mark's resume was put forward by the agent to the organization. The organization accepted him without further interviews, based on the agent's recommendation. Before the completion of the contract, Mark was offered and accepted, a full-time permanent job with the organization.

This is a good reminder that regardless of your experience with recruitment agents, use your newly honed powers of empathy to step into their shoes each time – they're just trying to do their job, how can you make their job easier? You never know when it might pay off for you.

Stay Accountable

Keep applying for new jobs and stay accountable. No matter how sure you are that this is the job and you are going to land it, just keep applying. Never pin your hopes on one application. Stay accountable to yourself or better still, someone else, by setting goals, and experiment with what works for you, for example:

- X hours per week searching for jobs to apply for
- X number of days to submit an application for every job you find (no waiting for the application closing date, you have X days to have the application submitted)
- Aim for X number of applications submitted per week

Once you start applying for jobs, it can become difficult to keep track of where you are up to with different jobs at different stages. Track jobs you've applied for by keeping a simple database, like the table below.

> You can download a free template for the Job Application Tracking database at www.whatnowcareer.com/resources

STEP 7 - The Secret Ingredients – Persistence, perseverance and preparation

Job Title	Due Date	Job Advertisement	Date applied	Status	Feedback
Title	Closing date	Copy & paste job ad	Date application sent	Not heard back, Unsuccessful, interview, etc	Record any feedback you received

Staying Resilient

When you face a protracted period of time looking for work and experience the accompanying rejections, it can be a challenging and stressful time. So, to normalize this for you, you may feel despondent, depressed, frustrated and despairing along the way. Here are some of the ways you can stay resilient throughout the process.

1. Remember it's a numbers game – and remember the numbers I've given you. If you're in the middle of writing the 11th job application and you're yet to be offered an interview, either you need to get some feedback and change how you're writing your applications, or you're likely to get an interview soon.

2. Change your success measures – stop judging the success of an interview on whether you land the job. Measure yourself instead on whether you have shown the best you in the interview. Give yourself credit for this – if this is the case, there is nothing more you could have done.

3. Protect your confidence – continually remind yourself that many of the reasons for being unsuccessful in landing a job have absolutely nothing to do with you. The rejection may feel personal, but in most cases, it's not about your competency or fit for the job.

4. Deal effectively with the feelings arising throughout the process, expect them and acknowledge their validity – anger, frustration, sense of unfairness and injustice. And when you can, label them and express them!

Support

Be kind to yourself. The skills we've examined in this book are built through practice. You're not always going to get it right and certainly not perfect from the start. It's not fair on yourself to expect to be naturally good at everything immediately.

Writing a good resume, writing applications, 'selling' yourself, operating well under a pressure situation such as an interview, answering questions on the spot – just look at the breadth of skill these encompass. And when you miss out on an interview or a job, support yourself by learning lessons and improving.

An external support network can also be enormously useful. Someone giving you moral support is invaluable throughout the process. Getting a job can feel isolating – you need or want the new job, you need to do all the work – it's you, you, you. Having someone 'in it' with you, to share your small wins and your ultimate win, and helping you manage the rejections and keep bouncing on to the next opportunity, is critical.

Accountability support can also help, to assist you to set targets and achieve. You know yourself best. Ask yourself the questions:

- What support do I need (and want)?
- What (and/or who) will help me keep on track?

You already know I wholeheartedly support and recommend getting assistance from a career coach, or a specialist resume writer etc. You don't *need* to develop all the skills needed, and often you're not the best person to keep yourself accountable. So, ask for help!

Celebrate your Successes

Finally, throughout all of your process, celebrate your success.

> *recognise and acknowledge your small wins along the way*

Of course, that's easy when you get to your ultimate aim – landing the job, or deciding on a new career, or doing something else you've decided you want to do. But don't forget to recognize and acknowledge your small wins along the way: writing a killer application that gets you an interview, when you really shine in an interview, and even just boosting yourself as you watch your self-awareness grow, your skills grow, and your tenacity get stronger. These little successes will be what help get you to your final destination, wherever and whatever that might be.

YOUR 'NOW WHAT?' ANSWERED

In some books, you can sneak to the final chapter and find out how it ends... I can tell you here how my big failure at job applications ended.

It has ended in this book many years later; but immediately after the failures, the insights in this book allowed me to re-evaluate my career goals and decide to go in a completely different direction and also to land the first job I applied for and the first step to my new career.

Unfortunately, I can't tell you how your story is going to turn out, but at least here is a cheat list for you. Paying attention to the following will mean you will have the most impact in reaching your 'Now What?'

- Spend time before *doing* anything to land a job, *thinking* consciously and subconsciously about what you want and need – you may be surprised where you end up

- Give the *Drop-Dead List* your complete attention at first, it will mean complete clarity later

- Do the *JAB* exercise, open to new ideas of what's possible, what you like and don't like

- Don't wait for jobs to be advertised, there are many ways to get the right job for you

- Tailor your resume, job application and answers to the selection criteria by paying attention to the person at the other end of them

- Interviews are a skill and skills can be learned

- Develop and use your empathy at every step – what does the recruiter want to see, hear or read? And remember, it's not about you, it's about them

- Time spent improving skills involved in landing your job will be well spent, but don't be afraid to seek help where it will make you more effective

- Practice, persistence, perseverance and preparation

- Never be afraid to ask for feedback

- Be you

> *Think differently to do differently*

Think differently to *do* differently, recognize the connectedness and potential of what you are doing, and simply keep going until you have achieved your 'Now what?'

Feel free to share your story by connecting with me on social media or my website www.kirstenbrumby.com

Connecting People to Purpose

Kirsten Brumby

ACKNOWLEDGMENTS

'Now What?' would not have been possible without all the people you have met through the course of reading it. They are all real people, though their names have been changed, and they all trusted me to help them along their respective career journeys. Many of them, and others I have coached along the way, I now count as friends. I have been privileged to work with them, and this book would not have been possible without my learning with them, and through their experiences.

My thanks also has to go to my publishing team who have allowed me to just write the book and made everything else so easy. Maggie, Trish, Carlos, Narelle and Mary Lou met everything I put forward with enthusiasm and encouragement, professionalism and a sense of humor.

Thanks are definitely due to my best friend and sisters, for letting me practice my career coaching skills on them at various times during their careers – Michelle, Mary, Steph and Rach. Finally, my gratitude to my inspiring family, Steve, Hugo and Heather, who take everything I do in my career, every change in direction, every dubious or wildly successful turn, in their stride.

MEET THE CONTRIBUTOR

**Alison Hernandez:
Director, Randstad Risesmart APAC**

Alison is a passionate, insightful thought leader on all aspects of change and transformation with deep expertise in career transition gained over the past 20+ years. She leads the Randstad RiseSmart business across Asia Pacific and sits on the global leadership team.

Alison is also a WGEA Pay Equity Ambassador, Retirement and ReCareer certified coach, Women's Agenda Award Winner 2014 and Stevie Gold Award Winner for Women in Business (Female Executive of the Year Asia, Australia, NZ 2017). A frequent speaker, media commentator and panellist on all topics relating to career and retirement, Alison is known for her energy, humour and incisiveness.

Having begun her career in the US in hospitality and quality management, Alison joined the UK Human Resources sector in the mid-nineties, subsequently relocating to Australia and finding a natural place for her skills and strengths in the career transition industry. A highlight of this time was developing and leading the Sydney 2000 Olympic Games career transition program for 2500 people. Having co-founded Sageco in 2004, she led the company acquisition in 2016 to become RiseSmart, the global career transition brand of Randstad Group, a leading global HR Services company.

Alison has a teenage daughter and lives in Northern NSW near Lennox Head, role modelling flexible work as a senior leader, commuting to and from RiseSmart offices across Australia, NZ and Asia Pacific.

REFERENCES AND RECOMMENDED READING

Books
1. Jeffers, S. (1987). *Feel the Fear and Do it Anyway.* MJF Books
2. Rock, D. (2009). *Your Brain at Work: Strategies for Overcoming Distraction, Regaining Focus, and Working Smarter All Day Long.* HarperCollins
3. Sandberg, S. (2013). *Lean In: Women, Work, and the Will to Lead.* Alfred A. Knopf

Articles
1. Mohr, T.S. (2014). *Why Women Don't Apply for Jobs Unless They're 100% Qualified.* Harvard Business Review
2. Tervooren, T. (2020). *The Art and Science of Making Great First Impressions.* https://riskology.co/first-impression/

MEET THE AUTHOR

KIRSTEN BRUMBY

After co-founding a consulting firm that generated seven-figures annually, Kirsten Brumby has spent over 20 years coaching, training and consulting for individuals, teams and organizations.

She specializes in helping people and organizations find clarity, set outcomes and achieve them. She has facilitated initiatives in leadership, small business, not-for-profit boards, career and life coaching; and has worked internationally across industries including corporate, government and not for profits.

Books by Kirsten Brumby

Now What?

A Step-By-Step Approach to Land Your New Job or Career

How to Write Effective Policies and Procedures

They System that Makes the Process of Developing Policies and Procedures Easy

Online Courses by Kirsten Brumby

- How to Write the Right Resume and Cover Letter
- How to Write a Job Application and Meet Selection Criteria (Secure that interview)

- How to Be Outstanding in Interviews and Land that Job
- How to Get Clarity About Your Next Career Move

Kirsten Brumby facilitates workshops and seminars internationally and is available for Keynote presentations.

www.kirstenbrumby.com

To download free resources from this book
www.whatnowcareer.com/resources

WHAT OTHERS HAVE TO SAY

"How can something so deceptively simple, be so life changing? This is by far the most useful book I've read on career planning. It feels like Kirsten is there with you offering support and encouragement all the way. A must have for jobseekers and career coaches!"

Francine Paton
Organizational Development Consultant

"Full disclosure: I've worked with Kirsten for over 20 years and I know what a great coach she is, so I was primed to expect a high-quality book. This book exceeded my high expectations. Kirsten's sharing of her own experiences and the stories of others takes what could be a dry subject and brings it to life. Rarely have I read a book that is in one package so practical, so engaging and so potentially life changing."

Howard Boorman
Writer, Facilitator, Coach and inveterate traveller

"I cannot recommend highly enough how Kirsten's career coaching strategies guided me from a place of uncertainty and confusion to my wonderful new career of nearly 3 years. This is no simple cookie cutter approach. Kirsten opened up possibilities and I found a new career I did not think would be open to me. The process of career coaching that I went through with Kirsten was instrumental in helping me make my own decisions to find the job I am in now.

At every step of the journey there were various tools and flexible strategies I could mould, use and revisit to keep me on the right path. Kirsten offered a personalized yet professional approach."

Vicky G
Accountant

"Working with Kirsten has helped me build confidence in myself. I now understand what I do and don't want in a job, and I have the tools to help me pursue the career of my dreams."
Ann-marie B
Award-winning Author

"Having someone who believes in you and encourages you is the best that you can get! With Kirsten's encouragement and guidance I've ended up achieving goals that I honestly thought were out of reach.

Kirsten is inspirational and because of her I didn't give up. I set goals and worked towards them to achieve personal greatness, and all due to her encouragement and guidance.

Kirsten made me brave. Thinking out of the box led to achieving goals that I never thought were within reach. Kirsten opened my mind to possibilities that I'd never considered and showed me that the only thing limiting me, was myself.

Kirsten took a dream and made it happen. She made me believe in me and pursue and achieve the unachievable."
Michelle Arnold
Executive Project Manager for Government

www.ingramcontent.com/pod-product-compliance
Lightning Source LLC
Chambersburg PA
CBHW071519080526
44588CB00011B/1482